BOYS
TO
MEN

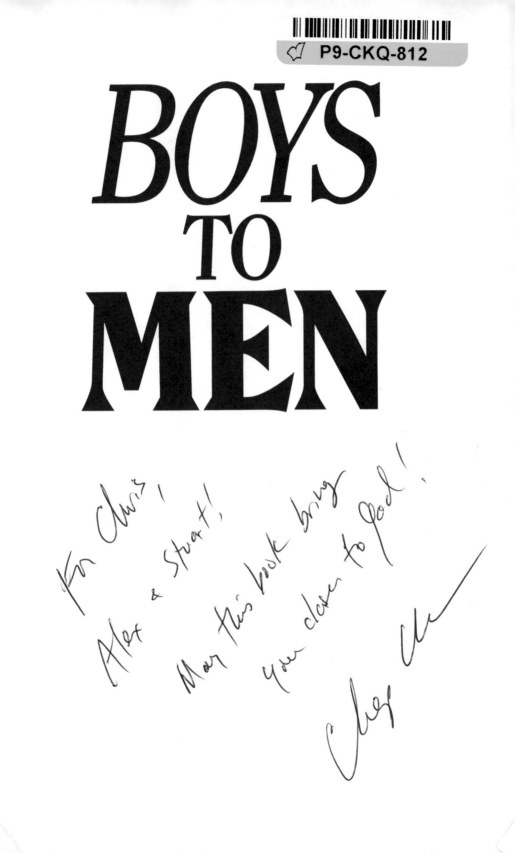

For Chris,
Alex & Stuart!,
May this book bring
you closer to God!.

HOW FATHERS CAN HELP BUILD
CHARACTER IN THEIR SONS

BOYS
TO
MEN

Steve Lee, Ed.D., and Chap Clark

FOREWORD BY GARY J. OLIVER, Ph.D.

MOODY PRESS

CHICAGO

To our boys becoming men:

Trevor and Ryan,
who are an enduring source of joy
and satisfaction to their father, Steve.
You teach me about life,
you challenge me to grow,
and you enrich my days.

Chappie and Robbie,
Chap's "Lion Cub" with a passion for life,
and his "Tender Warrior" with a gentle
and free spirit that captivates
all whom you touch,

and to Burt Ingersoll,
who taught me what it means to love
my Lord, my wife, and my ministry.
I'll miss you, Burt.

CONTENTS

MAN TO MAN

FOREWORD

As a father of three boys, my greatest desire is to see my sons grow up to become men who know, love, and follow Jesus Christ as their Savior and Lord. One of my greatest challenges is knowing how to help them navigate the journey from childhood, through adolescence, and into manhood. How do I develop character in my boys so that they become more than just men—so that they become godly men?

That's a question many fathers are asking today. As general editor of the Men of Integrity book series at Moody Press, I've heard confused, frustrated, and discouraged fathers ask:

Is there a map to help me understand where my teenage son is and what's happening in his life?

How can I help my son manage the rapid changes of adolescence?

Does adolescence have to be terminal?

Can I be his father and his friend?

How can I let go of my teenager so that I can receive him back as a young man?

How can I help my son become a godly man?

I've asked many Christian leaders about the key issues men face. Over and over again they told me a resource was needed to help fathers answer the above questions.

Fortunately, *Boys to Men* will answer those questions. Professors and youth speakers Steve Lee and Chap Clark have written a remarkable book that breaks new ground in raising sons. *Boys to Men* is based on the clear teaching of Scripture, and is supported by some exciting new research. It's also written in a style that is easy for men to understand and apply.

This book will help fathers to understand their sons' stages of development and their boys' specific needs in each stage; it can become a guidebook for raising your sons. If you want to raise sons in a way that will build character and move them toward spiritual maturity, then *Boys to Men* is for you.

GARY J. OLIVER
Author of *Real Men Have Feelings Too*

ACKNOWLEDGMENTS

In writing a book about fathers raising their sons to become men, we must acknowledge the help of many men in our lives, some much older, others are peers. Without their input in our lives, both in the past and now, we could not tell the stories of hope or offer the guidance contained in this book.

I (Steve) am deeply grateful to my dad, Wallace Lee, for the lessons he has taught me about life as I grew up and for the support he continues to give me as his son. I also thank Gary Oliver, my good friend, for believing in me as well as this project. He has been a model to me of what it means to love God and to love life. I cherish the times we have been able to spend together. Denny Miller, my pastor and friend, has contributed many ideas through his solid biblical teaching. And Cliff Miller has provided his gracious hospitality, helpful comments on the manuscript, and energizing yogurt pops.

I (Chap) thank my dad, John Clark, for his faithfulness and support, which continue to strengthen me as a man, a husband, and a father. Thanks, too, to my father-in-law, John Carlson, the most gentle man I have ever known.

We also are grateful to our wives, who have given much to this project and our lives. To Twyla Lee, thank you for your love and patience through the countless hours spent developing this manuscript. I can always depend on you when it seems like there is no one else. You're a priceless treasure to me and a magnificent mother—a gift from God. To Dee Clark, thank you for walking beside me in this journey of faith. You remain my wife, my friend, and my partner in all things.

Steve also acknowledges the assistance of Julia Dettmer. You always tracked down my requests for information and research data with speed and a smile. My thanks also to Warren Kaestner and Michindoh Ministries for providing a perfect setting to write.

Finally we want to thank Jim Vincent, our editor at Moody Press, for his careful attention to detail, his fine work in clarifying our ideas, and his gentle prodding that moved this project to completion.

INTRODUCTION

E ight-year-old Quinn was asked what he thought it feels like being a grown-up. "I think a lot of them feel like they wish they were young again so they can have a lot of good times. But most kids like me can't wait until we are grown up. . . . Maybe the people in-between got it best."[1]

To listen to common wisdom, teenagers—those "people in-between"—have it worse than most others, not better. The teenage years are often seen as a hurricane in the sea of life, marked by rebellion and defiance that cut a path of damage through the lives of parents who find ways to take shelter and wait for the storm to pass.

Bashing teenagers is common. Pointing out their faults and immaturity is easy if that's where you choose to focus. But our perspective on teenagers is similar to asking whether a glass is half full or half empty. Do you see your child's great potential?

Many parents, perhaps including you, realize that teenagers have many wonderful strengths. They can have a zest for life that is powered by boundless energy. Their sense of humor is often witty, and they can be fiercely loyal. They are generally more responsible than not, and their sense of fairness can bring strong reactions to injustice.

Showing you the positive side of adolescence is one reason why we wanted to write this book. We scan the adolescent landscape and see tremendous potential in our Christian young people. They are so alive!

But there is another reason, a bigger reason, why we wanted to write this book. We share a growing burden for the creation of Christian integrity and passion in adolescents, especially in our own boys.

This burden has led both of us into working professionally with adolescents and those who are preparing to work with them.

Many educational programs train men and women to minister to youth, and such training has tremendous value and is necessary. But they do not replace you, the parent. Parents are, and always will be, more effective in drawing their children to a vibrant relationship with Christ than will be their youth minister or other Christian worker.

FOR MOMS, TOO

This book is directed to fathers, specifically fathers raising their sons. But we want to welcome those moms who are interested in what we have to say. We're glad you're along for the ride! You, too, are a vitally important part of your son's world. We believe you will find that a lot of the information and suggestions given for each stage of adolescence can help you in your relationship with your teenage son. (See the appendix for some special pointers on raising your sons.) Our purpose in writing to dads is not to neglect nor downplay the impact you have as a mother, but there are some things that we want to say to dads in particular.

For boys, we believe that the communicated and passed-on faith of their father is a very significant factor in building a man of God. While we know a number of men whose spiritual journey has been stimulated and nurtured by men other than their father, a godly father who models spiritual vitality and disciples his son for the first eighteen years of his impressionable life remains a powerful force.

WHAT YOU'LL FIND

If we can help our sons—our future Christian men—to develop godly character and integrity in their formative adolescent years, then a transition to spiritual maturity and leadership in adulthood will be more probable and effective. With that goal in mind, this book will help you to: (1) understand the normal developmental stages and dynamics that your son is (or will be) experiencing, (2) relate to your son in ways that maximize a healthy relationship, and (3) implement some intentional strategies that will mark his journey to godly manhood in a meaningful way.

In Part 1, "Turning Boys Into Men," we set the stage for working with our sons. How committed are we to doing what we need to do in order to help our son become a man of God? What are the pressures and challenges that he will face in the coming decade? What do we know about how faith develops, and how can we use that knowledge to disciple our son in his faith? Finally, how can we help our son to mark his development toward manhood and becoming the adult that God wants him to be?

In Part 2, "Charting the Adolescent Years," we have divided the adolescent years into three stages. For each stage, we explore the ways our sons think, the challenges that are typical at that age, and how they relate with family and friends. We close by offering some suggestions for how to celebrate the end of each stage by marking it as a completed step on his march to manhood. Each of these "playbooks" should help you in choosing activities and strategies that will move your boy toward manhood.

It might surprise you that we have chosen to describe early adolescence as ages ten to thirteen. For better or worse, children at this age are definitely beginning to feel the pressures and challenges of adolescence. The past few generations have seen the age at which puberty begins creep down into this younger age group, and the influences and messages of society also accelerate the onset of adolescent issues.

On the other end, we do not mean to imply that we can turn out a full-fledged, "finished" adult at the age of eighteen. Our sons still have a lot of growing to do as young adults in their late teens and early twenties, but we believe that our effective role as parents who can provide discipling is coming to a close by the end of the late adolescent stage. We may still be an abiding influence in our son's life as he moves into adulthood, but it should now be more as a fellow believer and friend rather than as a parent.

In Part 3, "A Faithful Father," we stress the powerful role that you play in your son's development, and then outline some principles and techniques for relating to your son and helping him to assume responsibility for his life.

WHY READ THIS BOOK?

Chap and I believe this book is important for every father who has a son. Here are six reasons you will benefit by reading this book:

1. You want to be a better dad for your son.

2. You are the most powerful influence in your son's life.

3. Your son needs the best father he can get—and that is you.

4. Good parenting is not as easy, but also not as complicated, as the experts often make it out to be.

5. You want to understand what your teenage son is experiencing.
6. Effective fathers have vision, and we want to help you develop that vision.

As we look briefly at these six benefits, it should become clear that you are both qualified and chosen by God to raise your son to manhood.

1. *You want to be a better dad for your son.* While they may be out there, we have never yet met a father who has said, "I really want to mess up my boy—I hope I do a lousy job of being a father."

Maybe someone in your life is quick to point out how you fail as a father. But if you are like most of the dads we have met, you are deeply aware of your shortcomings and failures—you don't need someone else to tell you what you already know. Maybe you yell at him when you get angry, you notice what he does wrong faster than noticing what he does right, you don't listen to him like you should, and you let life crowd in on you and squeeze him out of your time. You kick yourself for being too hard on him or blowing chances to spend time together. You love your son, but you're not perfect. In spite of all this, deep down you want to be the best dad you can be. And that's where we need to start.

Desire to be a better father for your son is the first step to growth and change in your son. We hope you have the desire.

2. *You are the most powerful influence in your son's life.* In the late seventies, the movie hit *Star Wars* had many viewers uttering a phrase given to the young protagonist, Luke Skywalker: "May the force be with you." As Christians, we know that "force." As a father, keep in mind that in the life of your son, you too are a powerful force.

You may doubt that truth, especially if your own father was typical. He may have been so busy living life for himself that he rarely had anything to do with yours. Or maybe your memories are of hiding in your room as your father came home drunk, wondering whether or not he would beat you that night. Whatever your experience was with your own dad, let us assure you that he was the "force" that showed you what it means to be a man.

Parents are the key to stimulating Christian growth in their sons, and the father holds a unique place in that process. As dad, you are the most significant person in teaching your son what it means to be a man. For a boy, the communicated and passed-on faith of his father is a vital factor in building a man of God.

For better or worse, you are impacting your son in a more powerful way than any other man. Believe it! Your son is counting on you.

3. *Your son needs the best father he can get—and that is you.* Over the years we have bought the lie that it doesn't matter who the male role model is in our son's life, so long as he has one. But the research evidence has been gathering to show just how important you are to your son's growth. You are the best father your son can get.

Unfortunately, many dads don't really believe that in their hearts. There is a vague sense in which we believe that our son's needs can be met by others and that a father's positive influence is worthwhile, but not necessary. Mom provides nurture, schools provide education, churches provide spiritual training, and peers provide identity.

Ken Canfield, who has been studying fathering issues for years, states, "Our particular children—we can name them by name—are gifts of the Lord. He did not give us the wrong kids, nor did He give them to the wrong man. That means that you are the only person whom He intends to father your children."[2]

It is up to you to decide what you do with that responsibility. No one else can fully take your place. If you choose to neglect your responsibility to your son and your relationship with him, you both lose. The sad fact is that the full impact of that loss may not be felt until your son is grown and gone—and you are left with the regrets of "if only."

James Dobson, noted psychologist and founder of Focus on the Family, likens the task of fathering and the passing on of our faith to our children to a relay race. The most important heritage we can give to help our son build character is faith in Jesus Christ. And as track coaches emphasize, relay races are won or lost in the exchange of the baton. Dobson reveals his passion as a father by concluding, "According to the Christian values which govern my life, my most important reason for living is to get the baton—the gospel—safely in the hands of my children. . . . everything else appears 'pale and washed out' when compared with that fervent desire."[3]

4. *Good parenting is not as easy, but also not as complicated, as the experts often make it out to be.* There are plenty of experts who are willing to tell you how easy raising a child can be. They can give you "three easy steps to raising a happy, healthy, well-adjusted child." Beware of cookbook approaches that give parenting recipes! Raising a child from birth to adulthood is not the same as mixing up a batch of chili.

On the other hand, some experts would lead you to believe that you need an advanced degree in psychology in order to be a good parent. "Be careful, or you'll damage your child's fragile psyche," goes the argument. We disagree! Healthy relationships with children that produce mature, responsible adults have been happening for centuries. How did they do it without all the experts around to tell them what to do?

We are not offering any guarantees in this book. Bringing teenage boys to godly manhood cannot be guaranteed by anyone's recipe. That is a choice your son will ultimately have to make for himself. But there are effective principles and guidelines that can go a long way toward making such growth more likely. We want to provide you with those biblically based principles that research has confirmed are typical of healthy parent-child relationships.

5. *You want to understand what your teenage son is experiencing.* While we have all been teenagers, we often forget what life was like then as we get older. Your son is on a no-return path to adulthood, and he will find bumps and confusion on this never-before traveled road.

We cannot be truly effective as a father without being able to step into our son's perspective and see the world through his eyes. Many fathers, including some writers, make the mistake of prescribing how we should relate to our sons without first understanding who they are. But understanding should always come before prescription.

We have arranged this book in such a way that you can zero in on your son's current stage of development. Get to know him—how he thinks, the pressures he faces, the social realities of his peer group, and how he looks at family relationships.

6. *Effective fathers have vision.* One of the marks of a real leader is the presence of vision. What is vision? There are lots of fancy definitions that have been given, but we think that vision is nothing more than a dream in action. We can dream about what we hope our sons become, but without taking action to help make that a reality, it's just a dream. We can also act without a dream. We relate to our son according to the events of each day as it comes, and hope that eventually it will all fit together in making him the man we want him to become. But when we dream about who we want our son to be, and when we take action to help make that dream come true, that is vision.

A man with vision is one who can see the big picture—he sees where he wants things to go, and he works to make that happen. He doesn't let the everyday distractions and setbacks get in the way of reaching for that ultimate goal. His eye is on the prize.

Without vision, we perish. We become lost in the day-to-day details that bog us down and prevent us from growing. The fact is, many dads are not doing what they need to be doing because they have no real vision for who they want their sons to be. How they relate to their son today is based on nothing more than how they feel that day. There is no vision for what their interaction with their son will mean in the future.

Godly fathering requires a vision of where we are going with our son. Stu Weber talks about vision this way:

> What makes a man? First, foremost, and above all else, it is vision. A vision for something larger than himself. A vision of something out there ahead. A vision of a place to go. A cause to give oneself for. . . . We imagine we find status and security in these things, when in fact there is no status or security if you don't have relationships. . . . It is the unseen world, the world of the spirit, the world of relationships, where we ought to be majoring in our provision. Matters of character, heart, spirit, integrity, justice, humility—the kinds of things that last.[4]

As Ray Seilhamer, the bishop of the United Brethren in Christ denomination, says "vision. . . keeps us going when the going is tough." And as a result of having vision, priorities will emerge—priorities that will provide a framework for making healthy decisions.[5] It should be clear that dads need a vision for where they are going with their sons.

A GAME PLAN AND SOME PLAYERS TO KNOW

Our destination, of course, is building godly character into our sons as we move them from boys to men. For this we will need a game plan. That's why you will find three "Playbooks," one for each adolescent stage, in chapters 7, 10, and 13. Here you'll find strategies and activities for important rites of passage to becoming an adult.

You will have the opportunity to meet many fathers and sons in the coming chapters. All are playing in this important game of turning boys into men. Four key players you will come to know rather well in this book are our sons. We'd like to introduce them to you now.

Trevor Lee is a typical, energetic sixteen-year-old. He loves people and has always been an outgoing, social kind of guy. He likes to mix it up with peers and parents alike, trading jokes, barbs, and comebacks. Ryan Lee is our inventive twelve-year-old. Like his older brother, he enjoys other people and social activities. However, he is also more reflective and enjoys spending time by himself. His time alone is usually spent in creative activity, with his mind taking him to imaginary worlds that generate interesting stories.

Chappie Clark (soon to be Chap as he enters high school) is a fun, popular, and diligent thirteen-year-old thinker. He combines a zest for life with a flair for the original in everything he does. He has been a somewhat natural athlete, yet he has not allowed his love for sports to consume him. Robbie Clark is now entering the early adolescent phase of life. His gentle and fiercely independent spirit comes out of a freshness of faith that still takes us by surprise. His off-the-wall humor and his willingness to freely give whatever he has brighten people's lives.

Finally, to help you in this challenging game of changing boys to men of character and godliness, we have included special side articles in several chapters, which will provide cautions and guidelines in the art of fathering. These guidelines, called "Man to Man," will help you to understand and help your son on the journey to becoming a man.

We begin that journey in chapter 1 by looking at two fathers who approached their fathering roles in different ways. Though they were known for their success more on the playing fields of America's largest stadia, the NFL's Jimmy Johnson and Major League Baseball's Tim Burke are also fathers. As we shall see, their success with their boys, like ours, is more important than any achievements on the job.

PART ONE
TURNING BOYS INTO MEN

Train a child in the way he should go, and when he is old he will not turn from it.
                              Proverbs 22:6

ONE

FOOTBALL, BASEBALL, AND RAISING BOYS

When Jerry Jones bought the Dallas Cowboys football team in March of 1989, one of his first moves was to fire the Cowboys' legendary coach, Tom Landry. Stepping into his place was Jimmy Johnson—a college coach who had won a national championship at the University of Miami.

Many Cowboys fans wondered whether he could be as successful in professional football, but Johnson was determined to make it, and in his intense desire to win football games he allowed little to stand in his way. As Johnson devoted most of his time to football over his family, his marriage deteriorated.

When he was offered the Cowboys' head coaching job, Johnson immediately said yes, even though his wife didn't want him to do it. Eventually he divorced his wife, Linda Kay; one observer noted that while their strained marriage might have ended anyway, "it was effectively terminated the night Johnson decided he wanted to coach the Cowboys."[1] In effect, he chose to make his career more important than his marriage and family.

Sports reporters and rival coaches talked about Johnson's enormous ego, and his confident swagger actually had people rooting against him, including some Cowboys fans. But over the next few years he led the Cowboys to two Super Bowl championships. His success has earned him a great deal of fame. Football is his life. But he has paid a price for his success.

FOOTBALL, BASEBALL, AND RAISING BOYS

"I don't think there were any mistakes raising my kids," he told *Sport* magazine. "Maybe there were things I'd have done differently, but they weren't mistakes. That's parenting." He added, "I almost treated [my sons] like players—very regimented. That's when I was there. I was gone most of the time."[2]

His sons will tell you the same thing. Once when Brent was late in coming home, Jimmy met him at the door and demanded to know where he had been. Brent answered by releasing years of frustration. He turned to his father and replied, "No, the question is, where have you been?"

Brent recalls the incident well. "It just bothered me that he would be gone all the time, and then he'd come back to town and lay down all these rules. I didn't think he was in a position to tell me what I can and can't do. So when he asked me where I'd been, I threw it back in his face."[3]

As men, we choose our passions and our commitments. Jimmy Johnson chose football. In contrast, Tim Burke chose family first, even though he, too, loves pro sports, specifically major league baseball.

Burke started playing catch with his older brother in their backyard as a toddler. He soon dreamed of playing major league baseball. His outstanding pitching skill allowed him to fulfill that boyhood dream, as he eventually played for three major league teams—the New York Mets, the New York Yankees, and the Montreal Expos. He was named to the All-Star team once and maintained a solid earned run average of 2.72 during eight seasons.

But the big drama—the major league decisions—were happening off the field. After Tim and his wife, Christine, tried to begin a family, they discovered that they could not conceive a child. After the Burkes grieved over that news, Christine wanted to adopt a child. Tim resisted the idea for some months, but then his heart began to change. Eventually, they ended up adopting four special-needs international children.

But Burke was not done with big decisions. His love for his wife and children moved him to make one of the biggest, and hardest, decisions of his life—the decision to give up professional baseball. After the 1992 season he had signed a one-year, $625,000 contract with the Cincinnati Reds. Now it was February 27, 1993, and the start of the Reds' training camp. He told his manager what he had decided, talked with some friends, cleaned out his locker, and walked away from baseball.

As Burke walked out of the stadium for the last time, reporters spotted the gifted athlete choking back his emotions and surrounded him, asking him why he was retiring. "Baseball is going to do just fine without me," he started. "It's not going to miss a beat. But I'm the only father my children have. I'm the only husband my wife has. And they need me a lot more than baseball does."[4]

Tim Burke was a successful pitcher in the "bigs." He had fame, money, and attention—he was living his dream. Then he walked away from it all.

"Many people have a hard time understanding how I could walk away from all the acclaim and the money that are such a part of major league baseball. . . . All my life I dreamed of being a major league pitcher. For eight wonderful seasons, I fulfilled that dream. Now I have a bigger dream. I want to be a major-league husband and a major-league dad."[5]

Jimmy Johnson, football coach, and Tim Burke, baseball player, both have a passion for winning. In their common passion they are like most men. We grow up seeing who can jump the highest, run the fastest, throw the farthest, and any number of other formal and informal everyday contests. As we grow, our desire to win is channeled in a variety of directions, but we still love to compete, and we want to win.

Johnson and Burke were dedicated to winning at the highest levels in their sports. They are men of commitment—they are committed to winning. The focus of their commitment, however, runs in different directions. By his own admission, Jimmy Johnson has, in many ways, made a decision to sacrifice his family for the sake of professional success and fame. Tim Burke has made a decision to sacrifice professional success and fame for the sake of investing his time and life in the development of his children.

Which of these two men do you admire more, dad? Where are you most concerned about winning? Are you drawn more to public success than to family success? Are you trying to win in the areas that are truly important?

Our Passions and Commitments

As men, we choose our passions and our commitments. Tough as it was, Tim Burke chose his family.

Whether you know it or not, you have made decisions about what is important. Your decisions are reflected in how you live your life, not in what you say. And your son knows what those decisions are—he can sense it. Most men have not sat down to think hard and make intentional decisions—the decisions have simply evolved over time, gradually taking shape and giving direction to who we are.

FOOTBALL, BASEBALL, AND RAISING BOYS

What decisions have you made? Do you want to see where your passions and commitments are? Then it's time for a little quiz to evaluate your "Father Time." Circle the number from 1 to 10 that best describes you for each of the following six items. Equal time with both should be scored as about a five or six. (Be honest with yourself—don't give yourself credit for what you wish you would have done).

FATHER TIME

During the past three months, I:

Spent time doing things with my friends— golf, bowling, going to a game.	1 2 3 4 5 6 7 8 9 10	Spent time doing things with my son—golf, bowling, going to a game.
Spent extra time with work activities to make my boss happier.	1 2 3 4 5 6 7 8 9 10	Spent extra time with my son's activities to make him happy.
Enjoyed talking with my friends or co-workers.	1 2 3 4 5 6 7 8 9 10	Enjoyed talking with my son.
Found energy for taking care of business when tired.	1 2 3 4 5 6 7 8 9 10	Found energy for doing something enjoyable with my son when tired.
Spent time helping at church, actively involving myself in ministry.	1 2 3 4 5 6 7 8 9 10	Spent time helping my son think about and grow in his Christian faith.
Became excited about my job or my relationships with friends.	1 2 3 4 5 6 7 8 9 10	Became excited about my relationship with my son.

Now add up all the numbers that you circled. A middle score, 26–34, indicates that you give equal time to your son as compared with other areas of your life. If your score is above thirty-four, congratulations! You most likely enjoy your relationship with your son and are investing yourself in his healthy development. If your score is below twenty-six, we want to encourage you to rethink your priorities and make some fresh commitments to your son. The choice is yours.

This book is written to dads who want to win as dads. In particular, it is written to dads who have sons who are (or will be) becoming men—a process that occurs primarily during adolescence. Our sons want and need our help to navigate the turbulent teenage waters successfully. They may not say so, and they may not even think so, but

FOOTBALL, BASEBALL, AND RAISING BOYS

deep inside they want our help. The problem may be in how we try to help. Our growing sons need us.

Remember the days when your young toddler was learning to walk? Dads and moms get pretty excited when that happens. As a father, you stood about ten feet away, encouraging your young bundle of determination to make the long journey from one to the other. As his eyes grew wide and he stumbled forward, you were there to encourage him and help him up when he fell. And there was no way for him to learn to walk without falling. Skinned noses and bruised knees were badges of effort, and eventually he gained confidence and learned to walk with skill. Your fatherly chest swelled with pride as you thought, *That's my boy!*

In a very real sense, adolescence is the toddler stage of adulthood.[6] Our sons' attempts at adulthood are pretty wobbly at first, and they often fall and scrape their emotional and social noses. But with praise and encouragement, they keep trying. If we hang in there with them— if we offer help and encouragement instead of put-downs and criticism —they eventually gain confidence and become more skilled in adultlike attitudes and behavior. Our job is to guide and encourage them to learn to walk as godly young men. To do this, we need to: (1) recognize how important we are in that process, (2) understand what our sons are dealing with as they move through this time, and (3) equip ourselves with strategies that we can put to use. That is why we are writing this book.

KEY TRUTHS ABOUT FATHERS

In the introduction, we discussed six ways reading *Boys to Men* would benefit fathers. Those reasons, on pages 13–17, reflect six truths about fathers. We want to amplify on two as you consider the challenge of being a good dad:

1. You are the most powerful influence in your son's life.
2. You can understand what your son is experiencing.

You may find it hard to believe you can be a vital force in the life of your son. Yet you will be with him for the rest of his life, just as your father is with you. He is part of your earthly family, and you will remain part of his identity.

Testimonies from thousands of men and findings from scores of studies all point to the powerful influence, for good or bad, of a father on his son. Our prisons are filled with men who carry heavy burdens of hurt and anger toward their fathers. Our homes are filled with men who don't know how to relate to their sons and provide them with the love and mentoring that they need because they never had a father who showed them what that looks like. The power of a father can last a lifetime.

Stu Weber, a pastor who leads marriage and parenting conferences across the country, understands the power of this fathering "force":

> The great river of fathering that leaped from the primordial mists of Eden rolls through time and into eternity. How will you bend the course of the tributary that flows in your family? You will affect it, you know. For good or ill. Whether you work at it with all your heart and soul or close your eyes and ears and put your hands in your pockets and pretend it doesn't exist, you will channel that river in one direction or another. That's the nature of fathering. You can't hide from its potency and power. [7]

Second, you can understand and contribute to your son's experience of growing into an adult. Adolescence is a unique time where the worlds of childhood and adulthood collide. If we want to impact that time, we need to understand the special dynamics that are at work in the lives of our sons. We must know our sons.

And you can, by exploring the three stages of adolescence described in *Boys to Men*. As you get to know your son, his thinking, his social development, and the pressures he faces, you can help him. Effective fathers seek such knowledge, as fathering expert Ken Canfield points out:

> There are two components to an effective father's knowledge of his child. One is a general knowledge of how all children grow and change. The other is a specific knowledge of who his children are as individuals. . . . The technical term for a general knowledge of how children grow and change is developmental awareness. . . . This developmental awareness might seem like so much book knowledge—something best left to child psychologists. But effective fathers actively seek out such knowledge. [8]

Here's one additional truth about fathers trying to rear sons: You need a game plan for relating to your son in order to help him grow to manhood. One of the marks of a winning coach is the ability to not only know and understand his players, but to develop and pass on to them an effective game plan. If we are going to help our sons to win, we need a playbook that helps us to relate with them in effective ways so that we can empower them to "play the game" well. Dads need to understand what their sons are going through as teenagers, interact with them in healthy ways, and give them some tools for becoming godly young men. The three playbooks in chapters 7, 10, and 13, as well as the discussions in Part 2 of how boys change in thinking and social needs, will help you to understand and interact more effectively with your son.

Playing to Win

Are you sitting in the stands, dad? It is time to come out of the stands and take your place as a player/coach. You need to be playing a role in the ministry of your church and your family. A man discovers the fullness of life when he opens his mind and his heart to using his God-given gifts, talents, and opportunities. There is joy in being an active participant in your son's growth. You need to be coaching your son in the ways of the game.

If we can help our sons—our future Christian men—to develop, explore, understand, and own the Christian faith in their formative adolescent years, then a transition to spiritual maturity and leadership in adulthood will be more probable and effective.

Tim Burke has decided that winning with his children is a game worth winning. We are committing ourselves to winning that game as well. How about you? Only you can make that decision—no one can make it for you.

TWO

GROWING UP MALE IN TOMORROW'S WORLD

When your father (and when your grandfather) first became a dad, he knew just what that role meant. The responsibilities of fatherhood were clearly laid out and defined in those days, at least for most men. There was a clear distinction between what was expected of a man and what was expected of a woman. The father's job was to teach his son a trade, assure him some level of education, and "provide and protect."

Today what it means to be a man, and just when the transformation from boyhood to manhood takes place, is up for grabs at best and culturally ignored at worst. But our sons still need to be taught just what defines a man. They need to know in what ways they differ from girls (and we don't mean just physically), what is expected of them as they grow, and to receive clear markers that tell them they are progressing in their journey toward maturity.

In addition to the need for clearly defined rites of passage that identify and mark growth, our sons, the men of tomorrow, need to be prepared to face unique challenges. Many of these challenges are ones that, as parents, we did not have to face. Parents committed to helping their sons grow into men of integrity must, first, understand what their sons will face as men, and second, recognize what characteristics they must possess to be a beacon of love and hope in a dark and hostile world.

DEVELOPING A GODLY MAN

For the Christian father, there is another need that is even more crucial than the first two: having criteria upon which to spur and evaluate spiritual growth and movement. In the past this seemed straightforward; a committed follower of Christ had regular church attendance and involvement. But the man of God is called to be far more than an attender and participant in a weekly worship service. What does it mean to grow up in the Lord? How do you lead a boy, with an accompanying "child-like" faith, to a maturity of faith in Jesus Christ which shapes his entire person?

The task sounds ominous. To prepare your son for Christian manhood in such a scattered society can seem an almost impossible undertaking. But there is hope! To help your son become the man God has called him to be is not beyond your ability or expertise. God would never give you this responsibility, and great privilege and honor, if he knew you were not up to it. In fact, God has personally chosen you to lead your son through the years of childhood with the goal of presenting him as a man ready to follow Jesus Christ on his own.

There will never be any guarantees, for the choice of whether to trust Christ ultimately rests with him. God is not calling you to total responsibility for your son's life. As David Howard, the General Secretary of World Evangelical Fellowship, has said, "As a father, I can teach my children, train them, and show them what they ought to do. I can give them a game plan, so to speak. But they have to get out into life and do it on their own. Realistically, I can expect my teens to do the best they can—but I can't do it for them."[1] But like the father in the parable of the prodigal (Luke 15:11–32), God *is* calling you to love your son with passion and integrity, and to be faithful. That is the task of the Christian parent.

Taking the thoughtful energy and focus to understand him and his needs is the first step in helping your son to grow as God's man. This involves helping your son understand three elements of becoming a man: (1) the uniqueness of what it means to be a man; (2) the nature of the world he will face as a man (to prepare him for that world); and (3) what defines biblical Christian maturity. Let's consider first what it means to be a man.

To Make a Man

When my son Robbie began his football career as an underweight nine-year-old, the first day of practice opened with a speech by his grandfatherly football coach. A large man with a strong "Texas twang" sat the eight- and nine-year-old boys down and, looking at his charges, said, "Boys, your fathers did not bring you out here to become pansies.

Do you know what a pansy is? It's a cute . . . little . . . flower. No, sir! Your fathers brought you out here to make you a man! There are no 'cute little flowers' on this team; only men!"

"Your fathers brought you out here to make you a man." What did the coach mean? What makes a man? Is it the camaraderie of the team experience? Is it the ability to hit harder and intimidate more than the eight- and nine-year-olds on the other side of the ball? Is it physical strength, courage in the middle of adversity, or not shedding tears? Perhaps, in our society, it is a combination of these, and then some.

Being the Man that God Intended

What does it mean to be a man? Many observers make major distinctions between what is "masculine" and what is "feminine," yet the Bible, especially the New Testament, is surprisingly silent. There are great models of men and women in Scripture who exemplify certain qualities, but these are more descriptive of individual people than ideals to be identified and categorized. Biblically, the movement from boyhood to manhood means simply to become the person God has created the man to be. As family psychologist Gary Oliver writes,

> It's time for us to become proactive, to be defined by who we are and who God has created us to be and to become. We should be defined by our person and not by our performance or our production. The essence of true manhood is not found in what a man does, in how big or strong he is, in how much money he has made. It is found in who he is and what he is becoming. It's found within his heart, his moral character, his values and integrity. It is found in personal characteristics such as courage, steadfastness, responsibility, duty, fortitude, generosity, and the fruit of the Spirit.[2]

Today it is as if being a man is somehow a mystery to be uncovered or an ideological stance to be defended—masculinity is under attack in our society. But God has already fully equipped your son to become the man He wants him to be within the context of who he is! If he is a gentle, artistic, or creative person (like my son Robbie), God may have created him to be more like a willowy deer than an aggressive battering ram. For either kind of boy, it is most important to help him to see that for him to become a man means to fall in love with Jesus Christ, and to allow himself to be changed into His image, just as he is. To try and make him into someone or something that he is not is not only useless,

31

it may do more harm than good by not allowing him to develop into the man God has created him to be.

Looking to Jesus

Our sons need to know that biblical manhood is always defined by character—character that is expressed through love. Jesus Christ exemplifies the kind of character that marks a man of God.

Jesus was kind, but He also was tough when he challenged the Pharisees. Jesus was humble, but he was confident when He spoke to the crowds. Jesus was gentle, yet he was powerful in how He stood up to the money changers. Jesus was a "man's man" in how He lived—with great courage, passion, and strength. Yet Jesus was also a listener, a champion of the lost and broken, and a man of great compassion for the sinner. He was willing to sit on a dusty road with a bleeding woman when the synagogue ruler needed His immediate attention, and He stood tall when falsely accused by the Sanhedrin.

Jesus Christ is our model of what it means to be a man. A man of character. A man of strength. A man of integrity. Our sons are called to become the same kind of men, men defined by their character.

The World Our Sons Will Face

We also need to help our sons understand the world they will face as men. Steve and I share a unique circumstance—we both have boys who will graduate in the year 2000. Every time we think of it, we cringe. When our children are high school seniors, they will walk down the hallways of their respective schools, wearing letter jackets that have two giant 0's. The class of 2000, or, as they said in 1900, "the class of double-aught." We don't know what their senior year in high school will bring, although we doubt they will zip to school on hovercraft or ingest pills that maximize their memory skills before a big exam. We do know, however, that things will not be the same as they are now.

We believe that every father must recognize that the world his son will face will be different in a myriad of ways. We can never fully know what kind of skills or knowledge our sons will need to succeed in the future. Even today, the average adult changes careers a number of times over the course of a lifetime. We can, however, help them to develop the character it will take to be a committed follower of Jesus in what many religious observers are calling an expanding "post-Christian culture."

What will life be like for our boys as they go to college, find a job, get married and raise a family? John Naisbitt, author of *Megatrends* and

GROWING UP MALE IN TOMORROW'S WORLD

Megatrends 2000, has stated that "We stand at the dawn of a new era. Before us is the most important decade [1990s] in the history of civilization. . . ."[3] With the information highway running at full speed, the resultant "cocooning," a label sociologists use to describe the movement to home offices and spending spare time inside one's home, and the fierce competition for the best, newest, and most cost-effective products and services, our boys are going to face an increasingly complex world. What kind of a world must we prepare our sons to handle as we seek to help them grow into a man committed to Jesus Christ with honesty, depth, and integrity?

Relationships

Virtually all "futurist" experts, advertising executives, and business leaders agree that the computer will forever change the way we live our lives. The advent of such technologies as the 500-channel interactive video network and the "information superhighway" is prompting these experts to predict a sweeping array of cultural and societal changes. As mentioned, "cocooning" is expected to drive a large percentage of the workforce home to work via modems and fax machines.

The move away from personal relationships and interaction will not be limited to the adult world. Television and video games have already become increasingly interactive, and will become more so. Video baseball played alone now competes for the attention of young boys with pick-up baseball games in the neighborhood. A father recently told how his son invited one of his friends over to their house for the day. To his dismay, they spent the majority of their time swapping and playing each other's video games! Even with two boys in the house, there were long periods of silence broken only by the beeps and sound effects of the games. As technology creates even more entertaining games at more affordable costs, we can expect this "video cocooning" to grow as well.

In this setting, your son will have fewer opportunities to know people and develop friendships, and his friendships generally will lack depth. With great confidence in how technology will change the way we do business, shop, and play, most of these experts fail to recognize the fundamental nature of human beings—the basic drive to love and be loved. We are first and throughout social beings, created to interact with our God and with each other. We are not primarily workers, merchants, consumers, artists, or computer junkies. All of our expressed talent and drive flows from the desire to find meaning and relevance in the world. Cocooning may appear to be the wave of the future, but it will never replace our need for relationships, for the personal touch.

This interpersonal need, especially among men, is finally beginning to show itself. The need among men for intimacy and relationships was first heralded by secular authors, such as Sam Keen and Robert Bly, who invited lonely and broken men to admit and embrace their need for friendship. The Christian men's movement, most notably expressed by the Promise Keepers conferences and seminars, has continued this awakening and far surpassed the influence of Keen and Bly by drawing together tens of thousands of men to stand together as men who value integrity in relationships and lifestyle. Though isolation from others may come, men do not seek such isolation from interpersonal interaction, as demonstrated by the popularity of the Promise Keepers movement in its call for men of different races and denominations to unite in loving, caring relationships.

Even as technology expands, enticing our sons to spend more and more hours in front of the television and video monitors and away from friendship and intimacy, we will need to train them to recognize that real life is experienced within the context of interpersonal relationships. Relational vulnerability, authenticity, and the ability to maintain and deepen friendships will be an important gift we give our sons for the years ahead.

Marriage

Depending on who one reads, traditional marriage is either on the ropes or is gasping its last breath. A traditional marriage is one defined as a couple that actually means what they promise in their vows. "I promise to love, honor and cherish you," the vows state, "in sickness and in health, for richer or poorer, for better or worse, until death do us part." Yet as the 1980s closed, the Princeton Religous Research Center found in a study of college students from one hundred schools that 56 percent believe in "trial marriage" and 69 percent approve of divorce in cases of incompatibility.[4] The implication is we live in a culture that says "I commit" until it is no longer comfortable or convenient or personally fulfilling to remain committed.

But the consequences of broken families are coming to light as family researchers allow the data to speak. Contrary to popular media reports and conventional cultural wisdom, there is strong evidence that boys raised without significant contact with their fathers, especially in a single-parent situation, develop insecurities and even hostile behaviors. Studies in the journal *Adolescence*, for instance, found that a "significant number of teenage drug users are raised in single-parent homes or in families where parents are absent due to break-ups" and that jailed teenage boys are "more likely to come from mother-only families."[5] In addition, "children who exhibit violent misbehavior in school were eleven times as likely not to live with their fathers," according to the *American Journal of Public Health.*[6]

Of course, this does not mean that all single parents will raise socially dysfunctional adults; God often gives grace and strength to mothers or fathers raising children alone. And many dedicated single parents are able to rise above the obstacles to raise healthy, capable kids. Furthermore, evidence suggests that the effects of divorce and the absence of the father can be overcome or at least smoothed out by the presence of a committed male role model. (We discuss the need for a male model and ways to do this in the appendix.) The point is that fathers are extremely important in the overall development of their son as they grow into adulthood. A family of divorce rarely, if ever, can produce as healthy an environment for raising children as a marriage that is committed to selfless and sacrificial love. Remember, God's design is for a committed, loving marriage as the laboratory for raising children.

A father's presence in the family is important to the child's well-being. As researcher Ted Bowman wrote, "A son's experience of his father, whether it is one of absence, neglect, presence or abuse, is a powerful one and directly impacts his sense of himself as a man and as a father."[7]

What does this mean for raising your sons? You and I must raise up a generation of boys who understand the importance and blessing of marriage, who recognize that real love means commitment. We can help them to understand just what they are promising when they get married so that they are willing to give themselves to their wives for life. True love can only flourish when it is nestled within the context of the security and trust of an unconditional commitment. As the years go on, our culture may continue to downplay and devalue "traditional" families and marriage. As Christian fathers we can prepare our sons to stand up as men of integrity with their wives and children. We can help prepare them to stand against a culture that may tempt them away from the covenant they make with the wife of their youth.

Church

As of this writing, small churches continue to thrive, yet at times they are eclipsed by big churches that offer more services and feature bigger budgets. The rise of the "megachurch" has its advantages, including causing many churches to become more "seeker sensitive," designing worship services that will be attractive to the person who is turned off to the more traditional service and yet is seeking spiritual answers. It also has made smaller churches evaluate their effectiveness. Both can exist, yet many wonder about the church of the future. Will it be bigger and less personal—or will it offer an attractive product that still presents the true message of the gospel?

Another changing distinctive of churches in America is the decline in denominational loyalties. A few years ago people went to the same church their parents and even grandparents attended, and, even if they moved, they sought out a church from the same denomination. Today we have become "religious consumers," moving from church to church, looking for better music, a more dynamic preacher, an active youth ministry program. Is this trend negative? It depends on who you talk to. Some believe that denominational loyalty is somehow more biblically legitimate, whereas others argue that a Christian must attend a church that meets his particular needs. The only thing certain is that the form, expression, and nature of church is changing, and will continue to change.

However you feel about the church of the future, there is a strong possibility that your son will attend a large, consumer-sensitive church that uses Sunday mornings to woo the disinterested and uninvolved. Even if he attends a church that emphasizes worship among believers rather than evangelism, for him to develop as a mature believer he must connect with the others who attend, as well as the leadership of that body. He must be willing to do more than show up; he must be encouraged to proactively receive teaching, support the ministry financially, and participate in the life of the body. This is God's call to the man of integrity. As fathers, we must help our sons to see that the Christian faith is expressed primarily through covenant relationships with other believers in the context of Christian community.

Though changes in relationships, marriages, and churches are inevitable, a number of other changes also will confront our sons in the soon-to-be future. How they handle those changes remains to be seen, but of this we are certain—a solid faith relationship with Jesus Christ is the best anchor they can have as they confront a rapidly changing world. In the next chapter we look at how to develop faith in your maturing boy and move him toward Christian maturity, the third and final step in becoming a man.

THREE

FAITH AND YOUR SON

How does a child's faith in God and in the Savior, Jesus Christ, develop over time? Several thinkers have proposed differing ideas and theories about how one's faith develops and people grow toward Christian maturity. Consider these two radically differing interpretations of how faith develops. James Fowler, who is well-known for his theory of faith development, believes that it is during the teenage years that faith begins to become an internalized rather than an externalized value. That is, kids begin to own their faith for themselves rather than for their parents or peers. Gordon MacDonald, on the other hand, has stated that "A high school kid is not interested in a radical commitment. Most high school kids who are interested in 'radical commitment' are really just rebelling against their fathers. It's a way of asserting their independence. The genuine radical commitment doesn't happen in the teen years."[1] So which is it? Every youth pastor that we know disputes both of these positions. And for dads who want to help their sons to grow in faith, understanding how faith develops would seem to be an important step, right?

When we first talked about this book, we felt it would be important to say something about how our faith develops. After all, that's a big part of what Chap and I both want to encourage in the lives of our own sons. For boys to become godly men, their faith needs to deepen and mature. So how does that happen? We believe that God's Word has much to say about how faith matures. What follows is a model drawn from Scripture that has helped us to gain some perspective on the development of faith and Christian character.

As our boys become men, we hope that this model will also be of help to you. We offer it as a new way of looking at faith development that we believe can shed some light on how to interact with your son and train him in a way that fosters his spiritual maturity.

We believe that an understanding of how faith can and should develop needs to recognize that the Bible is filled with truths that don't seem to make much sense yet are true. Three of these truths are: (1) we are to have a simple faith, like that of a little child; (2) we are to grow beyond simple faith, pursuing a faith that is deep and mature; and (3) having a faith with childlike simplicity and mature complexity at the same time is not only possible, but ideal.

TRUTH AND PARADOX

We will consider each of these truths after we consider the idea that biblical truths don't seem to make much sense. We emphasize that they "don't *seem* to make much sense." Bible truth is still truth. The complicating factor is that paradoxes—situations that seem to contradict each other—are still true.

The Bible is filled with paradoxical situations. For example, consider how the following biblical truths work:

- We find life by losing it.
- Whoever is first will be last.
- Christ is fully God, and Christ is fully man.
- The greatest among you will be a servant.

As Jesus taught and lived these and many other seeming contradictions, the "great minds" of his day found them confusing. The apostle Paul once wrote, and it remains true, "the message of the cross is foolishness to those who are perishing" (1 Corinthians 1:18). Human logic will always leave us confused in trying to understand the nature of God and the mysteries of the Christian faith. Biblical truths can seem like contradictions. The above examples and many other statements like them leave us scratching our heads, puzzled by what seem to be irreconcilable differences. But from God's point of view seeming contradictions are not contradictions at all.

When it comes to faith development, we meet the first of our three major paradoxical yet profound truths. On the one hand, Christ taught us that "unless you change and become like little children, you will never enter the kingdom of heaven" (Matthew 18:3). Apparently our faith is to look like that of a small child. Even as adults we can only become Christians by having the faith of a child.

Such faith is simple. Look at the faith a small child places in his own father. Maybe you've heard your son say, "Let's take it to my dad, 'cause my dad can fix anything," or "My dad can beat up your dad." That's the unquestioning, simple belief in the power and sufficiency of a dad.

Similarly, when a child comes to Christ, all he knows is that Jesus loves him and that He died so that his sins can be forgiven and he can go to heaven someday. The gospel is that simple. It does not require an educational degree or advanced thinking to commit to following Jesus Christ.

On the other hand, we are admonished to "become mature, attaining to the whole measure of the fullness of Christ. Then we will no longer be infants, tossed back and forth by the waves" (Ephesians 4:13–14). Growing in our faith is expected. "Anyone who lives on milk, being still an infant, is not acquainted with the teaching about righteousness. But solid food is for the mature, who by constant use have trained themselves to distinguish good from evil" (Hebrews 5:13–14).

Here two truths seem to bump heads. How can we have a simple faith and yet be commanded to develop a maturing faith? The mystery and depth of what it means to be a Christian and to mature in our faith is complex. Yet we are commanded to grow in our understanding.

No matter how many times we read God's Word, we can never master its content nor plumb its depths. We gain new insights each time we come to it. Theologians have been debating various biblical issues for centuries. Like us, they can continue to learn and to grow in their faith. God works in our life to enrich our understanding of who He is and who He wants us to be.

Childlike Faith, Complex Faith

Simple childlikeness and complex maturity. Scripture seems to value both. Faith should be like that of a little child, and yet faith must be mature. But how do we remain childlike and mature at the same time? It has to be one or the other, doesn't it? After all, simplicity and complexity are opposites, right? Something cannot be two opposite things at the same time. A room cannot be light and dark at the same time. Food cannot be fresh and spoiled at the same time.

FAITH AND YOUR SON

Understanding comes when we realize that something can be simple and complex at the same time. An example will help to make this clear.

When you get right down to it, football is a simple game. You need for your team to get the ball, move it down the field with various plays, score more points than the other team, and do all of this within some basic rules. Simple. Chap and I both started playing football at a young age, and, as kids, neither of us felt that it was all that difficult a sport to master.

As we got older, however, the game got more complicated. Today, my (Chap's) boys are both playing football as we write. Chappie, age thirteen, is in his third year, and Robbie, nine, is just starting. Robbie's team, a first-year tackle team, has a few basic plays—sweep left, sweep right, up the middle, a pass play. Sometimes the greatest challenge for the coaching staff is to get the kids to understand the concept of "the line," for to a nine-year-old a line is when you get behind somebody! The game is basically reduced to blocking, tackling, and not getting yelled at for picking flowers.

Chappie, on the other hand, is part of a machine-like organization. These junior high boys need to be able to distinguish several different offensive formations, complex defensive schemes, audiblized blitz commands, and memorized hand signals from the bench. These boys, though only a few years older, must not only remember to block and tackle, but they are expected to execute as a unit as well. Robbie would be totally lost on Chappie's team. Football, though simple in essence, gets more and more intricate and complicated at each level of competition. Simplicity and complexity—football is both at the same time. So is our faith.

One of the mistakes we make is to assume that simplicity must be lost when faith deepens and becomes more complex. In part, this is what seems to be missing in most theories of faith development. We do not need to lose touch with the childlike simplicity of our faith as we get older and our faith becomes more complex, more mature. Faith is not a case of "either-or," but of "both-and." God desires our faith to be both simple and complex, childlike and mature. The apostle Paul affirms this dual understanding of faith when he encourages the believers in Corinth, "In regard to evil be infants, but in your thinking be adults" (1 Corinthians 14:20).

A Simple Faith

Six-year-old Johnny has grown up with the benefit of Christian parents who love and nurture him. He has watched dad and mom sing in church, pray, and read the Bible. He wants to be like his parents, and you can see it in the way he attempts to copy their faith behaviors. He folds his hands and closes his eyes to pray, he opens the hymn book to the right page number and tries to follow along as best he can. When asked how he knows that God is real, he says, "I don't know, but He is." Johnny is a good example of what childlike faith looks like: trust and imitation.

Children who live with love demonstrate an anchoring sense of trust in their parents. They don't need complicated explanations. If dad and mom say something is true, then it is true. This is the starting point of faith—the simplicity of childlike trust in the love and power of God. This is not just an important idea to consider. Jesus Himself taught on the need for trust when He comforted His disciples, "Do not let your hearts be troubled. Trust in God, trust also in me" (John 14:1).

A simple faith is not only trusting, it imitates those in whom the trust is placed. We imitate the role models in our life. There is nothing wrong with imitation. It is said that imitation is the sincerest form of flattery.

Like Johnny, all children imitate their parents. From the time children are small, the faith of their parents is the standard to which they try to measure up. They want their parents to be pleased with them and approve of what they do. It can be humorous to watch the same mannerisms and behaviors in a child that mirror those of his parents (and sometimes downright humbling!).

Paul urges us in Ephesians 5:1 to "be imitators of God, therefore, as dearly loved children." In speaking to the Corinthian church, he tells them, "You do not have many fathers, for in Christ Jesus I became your father through the gospel. Therefore I urge you to imitate me" (1 Corinthians 4:16). The writer to the Hebrews goes further when he says: "We do not want you to become lazy, but to imitate those who through faith and patience inherit what has been promised" (6:12). As Christians, we are to be little Christs. We never outgrow our need for godly examples. The imitation of godly examples is part of our faith experience. Imitation is part of the simplicity of our faith. The evidence is overwhelming that the faith of a child is most often the legacy of the imitated faith of a parent.

A Complex Faith

The complexity of our faith is acquired by asking questions and digging deep to find the answers. Thinking about the mysteries of our faith and the hard questions of life can lead us to search out the answers.

The first four chapters of the book of Proverbs encourage us to seek wisdom. We are to search out the richness of God's truth and come to grips with the questions of life. "The fear of the Lord is the beginning of knowledge, but fools despise wisdom. . . . Wisdom is supreme; therefore get wisdom. Though it cost all you have, get understanding" (Proverbs 1:7; 4:7). Our faith must grow and become deeper—more complex.

So we are called to a faith of paradox—faith that is both simple and complex. The simplicity of our faith can vary in strength. And that is what you can expect in a son (and a daughter, too). We want to lead our children to Christ. If we do, we rejoice, for their spiritual salvation is secure, and they have begun a lifelong spiritual journey, marked by meaning in serving God and knowing the security of unconditional love. Yet, just like you and I, their faith can range from being weak to strong. The complexity of their faith can range from being low to high. If they have never wrestled with why they believe what they do, if they have never struggled with finding answers to the hard questions of life, the complexity of their faith will remain low. On the other hand, if your son has grappled with the difficult issues of life and faith, the complexity of his faith will be high.

A FAITH MODEL

Let's take a look at how these factors can combine. The types or levels of faith can vary, and they fall in one of four categories. (Notice the model of faith on the next page.)

Neglected Faith

As much as we would desire a problem-free life for our children, we must let them face those tough times. Remember, it is when they wrestle with why they believe that their faith can mature. Consider the story of Ben. Heavily recruited to play baseball, Ben enrolled in a small Christian college that was interested in his shortstop skills. Ben came from a home where God and religion were absent, and he soon began to feel out of place. Other students would freely talk about their faith, he went to chapel (as required), and professors would relate their courses to a Christian perspective. Not willing to put his trust in the God they presented, and not willing to engage in discussions about the Christian faith, Ben dropped out of school and enrolled in a state university.

Ben is a good example of what we have chosen to call *a neglected faith*. A neglected or absent faith is characterized by a lack of trust and commitment to the basic truths of Scripture and a weak or absent imita-

A MODEL OF FAITH

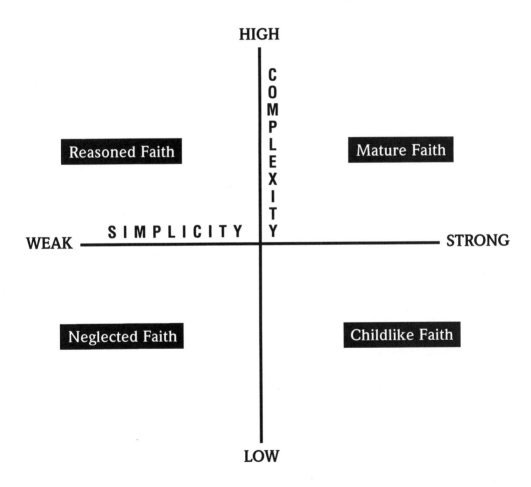

tion of godly qualities and behaviors. There is little or no questioning or thinking about the Christian life. This style is typical of a person who does not know Christ or has neglected his relationship with God.

Childlike Faith

Heather enrolled at the same Christian college as Ben, but she came with a strong commitment to her faith in Jesus Christ. Her parents were pillars in their small rural church, and she had been in church whenever the doors were open, or so it seemed, for the first eighteen years of her life. She planned to become a missionary, and she quickly involved herself in a student Bible study group. Her faith was strong and passionate. Heather was a spiritual leader on campus, as she modeled a godly lifestyle for others to see—a lifestyle that she had originally learned to imitate from her parents.

However, Heather soon became uncomfortable with some of the questions raised in her classes and the opinions of other students on campus. Encouragement from professors to think about her faith and to ask questions about why she believed what she did was not welcomed with enthusiasm. She didn't know what to say except that she trusted God and what the Bible had to say. She wasn't sure how to answer when asked about different Bible passages that seemed to say opposite things. She had never really thought about such things.

Heather is a good example of someone who has *a childlike faith*. A childlike faith is characterized by a personal commitment to follow Christ and live a life that will be pleasing to Him. The emphasis is on trusting God, obedience, and doing what God commands: "If you love me, you will obey what I command" (John 14:15). The faith of a child is trusting and spontaneous. This is the style of faith that is available to all, and can be nurtured in our sons from the time that they are little. We want to provide them with godly examples that they can imitate. In part, the Christian life does involve simple obedience that is motivated by love.

Many people who have grown up in the church and accepted Christ at a young age live this style of faith. They have been surrounded by Bible stories and easy answers for most of their life, and seldom have they felt the need to question why they believe what they do.

For those with a childlike faith, theological training or education that causes one to think deeply and critically about their faith can seem to be dangerous. Such training can create confusion or take the "fun" out of faith as they learn terms and concepts that are complex. Such learning may even seem unnecessary. "After all, shouldn't the Christian life be accepted at face value; you, know, by faith, not reason?" they seem to ask.

We don't want you to get the wrong idea. There is much virtue in a childlike faith. There is something attractive about a trusting, innocent obedience to Christ. There are many wonderful, godly people with a childlike faith whom God uses to touch the lives of others. The strong simplicity of this style is to be admired, not scorned. A strong, simple obedience to Christ and His will is something that we want our sons to carry with them throughout their lives.

Reasoned Faith

Like Heather, Dave had grown up in the church. He accepted Christ as his personal Savior when he was ten years old. He enjoyed studying the Scriptures, and he liked to think about biblical and moral issues. He took every opportunity to involve himself in discussions and debates about theological matters, stimulated by the exchange of ideas that occurred. Service opportunities and prayer meetings didn't really interest Dave much—he would rather get into a good intellectual discussion. He loved to think, and he had a tremendous amount of head knowledge about the Bible and Christian living—he just had a hard time living it.

Dave's faith is *a reasoned faith*. A reasoned faith is characterized by a complexity of thinking. There is an interest in understanding and gaining knowledge about one's faith. The ability to think about faith in this way is not really possible until adolescence. It requires a capacity to think in the abstract—considering ideas, possibilities, and values. This kind of thinking is mentally stimulating and challenging. Jesus stimulated and challenged the thinking of both his disciples and the people who came to hear him. He would often speak in parables, forcing his hearers to think about their meaning. At other times he would ask penetrating questions that prompted an inward search for the answer. Along with a simple, childlike faith, Jesus wanted his disciples to think about their faith and to understand their position as disciples.

In some ways, those with a reasoned faith can become similar in their faith to the Pharisees of Jesus' day. The Pharisees were educated men who loved to study and debate the intricacies of the law. They were theologically sophisticated, but, due to their arrogance, they lacked an appreciation for the beauty and simplicity of a childlike faith.

To those with a reasoned faith, the childlike style seems naïve. There is a sense in which they may feel superior or more advanced than their childlike brothers and sisters. Sadly, they run the risk of losing the innocent passion and enjoyment that comes with simple obedience that springs from a love of the Savior. They can be so focused on knowledge of their faith—doctrine and its implications—that they neglect or dismiss the need to maintain their personal relationship with Jesus.

Persons with a reasoned faith have accepted Christ as Savior, but are often more interested in thinking about their faith than living it. They can talk a good game and sound theologically sophisticated, but the simple faith of childlike obedience is weak. They mistake sophistication and complexity of thought for maturity.

Mature Faith

The simple trust and obedience of a childlike faith and the complex understanding and depth of a reasoned faith are both valuable. But neither one by itself is complete. A *mature faith* is characterized by a blending of childlike and reasoned faith. There is a strong commitment to a simple imitation of Christ and obedience to His will, combined with a thoughtful consideration of one's faith. There is a well-rounded integration of both the simple and the complex. The simple gospel message remains clear, while the biblical call to pursue wisdom and understanding is honored. Those who are mature in their faith are those who walk humbly before God in simple obedience, imitating the example of Christ, while also having a strong desire to gain wisdom and depth of understanding. That desire spurs them on to dig deep into the Scriptures, asking questions that challenge their faith to new levels.

This style of mature faith was beautifully illustrated in one comment by Karl Barth, the Swiss theologian. Barth was a prolific writer of theology and Christian living. His office was filled with books—many of which he had written—that examined and probed the Christian life from every angle. He sat in his office to be interviewed near the end of his life, surrounded by all of the wisdom and thought in his books.

The interviewer asked him what was the most significant thing he had learned in all of his years of study and writing. Barth pondered the question for a moment, and then, surrounded by a lifetime of thinking, leaned forward and said, "Jesus loves me, this I know, for the Bible tells me so." Simplicity and complexity. That is mature faith.

IMPLICATIONS FOR DADS

So how can this understanding of what faith should look like help you as you interact with your growing son? First, you need to be a Christlike example of mature faith. Your son needs to have an example

46

that he can imitate. Second, you need to look for opportunities to help your son think about his faith while encouraging a committed and genuine lifestyle which is characterized by an obedient and humble spirit.

Discussing real life from a biblical point of view is a marvelous way to stimulate thinking that will enrich your son's understanding of how to walk with his God. For example, how about some time discussing the following questions:

- What does God have to say about peer pressure?
- What behaviors honor Jesus Christ and my girlfriend in a dating relationship, especially in terms of sexuality?
- Why does God allow suffering in the world?
- How could God send someone to hell if He really loves everyone?
- Why does God allow things like child abuse, violence, and poverty?

The list could go on and on, but we believe questions like these will help you to develop in your son a genuine, committed faith that is both simple and complex, reasoned and mature. Not only can you enrich your son's thinking by talking about such questions, but you'll be deepening your relationship with him at the same time. Some of the most enjoyable times that we spend with our sons are when we are discussing these kinds of issues.

We can see some of you dads out there cringing at the thought of having discussions like this. One of the reasons why some dads resist encouraging their sons to think and reason about their faith is that they have not done it themselves. The fact is, dad, that if you are never encouraged to think deeply about your faith, you are probably threatened by the idea of having your son do so. However, when we don't encourage our sons to think, in a sense we rob them of training that will deepen their faith. A father who wants his son to have a mature faith will need to take the risk of developing the reasoned side of his own faith as well. "The heart of the discerning acquires knowledge; the ears of the wise seek it out" (Proverbs 18:15).

Our sons face an uncertain future. What it means to be a man in tomorrow's world is tough to answer. While we cannot fully anticipate all of the challenges that our sons will face, one thing is certain—God's love for His children is trustworthy, His Word is timeless, and His desire for bringing our sons to godliness is clear. If they are growing into

47

the person God calls them to be, if their character and maturity are grounded in an identity with Christ, God's faithfulness will see our sons through whatever trials and challenges the future will bring.

It truly is more important who are sons are than what they do. It is our task as parents to help them move to godly maturity, a maturity that demonstrates a childlike trust in their Savior, an obedient walk with their Lord, and a thirst for exploring and understanding the mysteries of their faith.

FOUR

FAMILY RITES AND RITUALS

We knew it was coming. We just didn't know it would come so quickly, almost, it seemed, in the twinkling of an eye. Our oldest son, Trevor, was now sixteen years old and ready to get his driver's license. It doesn't seem that long ago Twyla and I were propping him up in bed, dressed in his cute little football outfit, with drool running down his chin. (I guess we could still do that, although I don't think he would drool anymore.) But to quote my son, now he had become "a man."

That afternoon Trevor and I headed for the driver's license bureau immediately after school. My stomach did some flips as we approached the building, realizing that I might not be the one to drive home (or anywhere else from now on). Indeed, about one hour later, Trevor left with a piece of paper that made it legal for him to drive. Thanks to his finely-tuned guessing abilities and well-coached driving skills, he now carried a driver's license in his wallet. He no longer needed us to get him where he needed to go. The days of being his regular chauffeur were over. The truth hit—he had traded in his fifteen-pound bicycle for a two-thousand-pound steel missile.

Many teens, and not a few parents, consider the obtaining of a driver's license to be an American rite of passage—a marker that signifies a major step toward adulthood. It certainly gives its owner new mobility. But is it really a marker of maturing, of moving from boy to man?

RITES OF PASSAGE IN AMERICA

We could consider several events as rites of passage in mainstream America. For our adolescent sons, some of the events shown below might qualify as rites of passage. Which of the following do you think would show your son has become a man?

1. Going on his first date
2. Going through a religious ritual (for example, a Bar Mitzvah for a Jewish boy)
3. Getting his driver's license
4. Graduation from junior high or high school
5. Reaching the magic age of twenty-one

Although each of these events is certainly significant, none truly qualifies as a rite of passage. Why not? Consider what happens before and after each of the above events. They are looked forward to, celebrated, and enjoyed. In some ways, they should mark movement to a new stage of maturity. But most teens are really not treated much differently once the event is over than they were before it began.

The lack of real rites of passage in America makes it difficult for a boy to know when, or even if, he becomes a man. While primitive rites may seem barbaric, their simplicity and importance is attractive to a boy who constantly wonders what he has to do in order to be treated like an adult, as well as to feel like an adult.

Yet such rites of passage and preliminary rituals are important to our sons (and daughters too), for they show our children the privileges, duties, and importance of growing into adults, and they help us as parents to motivate and shape our children as they move toward adulthood. A final rite of passage gives the initiate the reassurance that he is now formally an adult. This chapter will look at how we as parents, particularly dads, can help our sons become men through the use of ritual.

SOME CULTURAL EXAMPLES

The methods that various cultures have for marking the movement from boyhood to manhood have been studied extensively. Here are just three examples.[1]

Boys of the Busama tribe in New Guinea do not need to guess when they become a man. The ceremony that marks that event is extreme, but well-defined. Men of the tribe first cut and burn them with sticks and firebrands as they make their way to their place of initiation. Bloodied by the ordeal, they are put in the care of two men who will oversee their initiation into manhood and teach them what it means to be a man. They are beaten, starved, and deprived of sleep and water. During this entire time they are instructed in the roles and responsibilities of being a Busama man. The initiation ends with an incision of the penis. The ceremony culminates in a series of feasts as the boy is now welcomed into the tribe as a man.

The ceremonies of the Arunta tribe of Australia seem just as bizarre to our American minds. They subject their boys to a rite of passage that involves burning branches being thrown at them, lying over an open fire on green branches, and a head-biting ceremony in which the men of the tribe bite deep into the boy's scalp.

In South Africa, Thonga boys must endure a three-month initiation ceremony into manhood. During this time they are beaten, denied water, and forced at times to eat such things as half-digested grass found in the digestive system of slain antelope. They sleep naked on their back in the cold nights, while being bitten constantly by bugs.

These rituals seem primitive, even barbaric, to our "civilized" society. And yet, these cultures have something that the majority culture of America does not—well-defined rites of passage that allow a boy to know when he becomes a man. As one young man grumbled,

> I wish I had it that easy. Run through the fire, step on the coals—then it's over and done with. You're a man, everyone knows that you're a man, and that's the end of it. For me it keeps on going and going. . . . The fire never stops; I keep running through it every day.[2]

The young man who made this comment recognizes two things that studies of various cultures have confirmed. First, ceremonies that mark the move to manhood reduce the confusion and struggle that often accompany that move. Second, America has no established ceremonies that truly serve this purpose, a fact that is lamented by a number of authors, as well as leaders in the current men's movement.

While they often involve painful events, such rites certainly make the journey to manhood a smoother experience for those cultures that have them. The rituals that boys pass through in these cultures are not just significant because of the separation or pain that is endured. They are intimately bound up with a sense of accomplishment, the achievement of an adult identity, a connection with adult society, and the memory of overcoming the obstacles needed to get there.

Marking the Territory

So just what is a rite of passage? The phrase defines itself. A rite of passage consists of two parts:

1. *Rite.* This is a form of the word ritual. Rites involve ritual, tradition, ceremony.

2. *Passage.* The idea of passage implies movement. In this case, it is a movement from one developmental status to another.

Rites and traditions are important parts of healthy family relationships, and they are particularly significant when they are given the special meaning of a rite of passage—when they are used to help a boy become a man. Let's take a look at each of these in more detail, particularly as they apply to our American culture.

Rites and Rituals

Do you open Christmas presents on Christmas Eve or Christmas morning? Do you always have turkey and pumpkin pie for Thanksgiving? How does your family celebrate birthdays? Are family devotions a daily tradition?

Healthy families have a myriad of traditions and rituals. In researching her book, *Traits of a Healthy Family,* Delores Curran discovered that a rich supply of traditions is one factor that distinguishes healthy families from unhealthy ones. She concludes, "Families who treasure their traditions and rituals seem automatically to have a sense of family. Traditions are the underpinning in such families, regarded as necessities, not frills."[3]

The value of rituals and traditions is seen in Scripture as well. The Old Testament is filled with ritual prescriptions that God gave to the nation of Israel. All of these rituals had symbolic meaning that represented God's relationship with His people.

Jesus also understood the power and importance of ritual. By His presence and participation, He validated the marriage ceremony, observed the Jewish festivals, and made a tradition out of eating with friends. He even instituted a new ritual for his followers, the ritual of communion, telling them, "this do in remembrance of me." Jesus performed the first communion during Passover, itself a ritual that God ordained as a reminder of His mercy in allowing the angel of death to pass over the homes of Jewish families, who had spread the blood of a lamb over their doorposts. Today communion is a powerful reminder to

FAMILY RITES AND RITUALS

us of Christ's love for us and the spiritual blessings we enjoy because of that work.

Yes, traditions and rituals are necessary and valuable pieces of our lives. Healthy families not only enjoy the inadvertent traditions that evolve, but they look for ways to intentionally create new ones that will be meaningful to their children as they grow.

Professor and author Tony Campolo, has echoed this call to celebrate ritual:

> Children from highly ritualistic families have an intense longing to identify with their families, and this longing leads them to find pleasure in doing those things that their families deem right. From a sociological point of view, parents who do not plan to have regular family devotions fail to take advantage of a practice that could mean the difference between having children who want to be loyal to the values and beliefs of their parents and children who readily abandon such beliefs and values. . . .
>
> There are so few things that can be controlled in a child's life these days that parents who neglect the use of ritual have neglected one of the few available instruments for building emotional security and loyalty to family values. When parents ask me how they can help their children to overcome insecurities, I answer, "Ritual!" When they ask me how they can get their children to embrace the right kind of behavior patterns, I say, "Ritual!" When parents ask how they can give their children good feelings about themselves, I say, "Ritual!"[4]

Does your family have a wealth of rituals and traditions? We hope so. They are the hooks on which we hang warm memories as adults. Even adults who came from destructive or hurtful families often report some bright spots in childhood, and those times usually involve some kind of family tradition. So develop and celebrate a legacy of traditions that your children can carry with them into adulthood.

MARKING A PASSAGE

A ritual that involves a passage will not simply celebrate what already is. The notion of passage means that an event is symbolic of movement—movement to a new developmental level and status. Throughout history, societies have devised elaborate ceremonies and rituals that mark movement, or passage, from childhood to adulthood.

Why go to all the trouble of devising such rites of passage? Why not just let boys become men in the normal course of events, and not mess with all the ceremonial trappings? Ray Raphael, a leading expert on rites of passage, gives us the reason.

> The salient feature of primitive initiations, and the reason they continue to hold such appeal, is simply this: They work. An individual who goes through an initiation comes out the other side with a heightened feeling of self-worth, for his manly status has been affirmed both to himself and to the group. His individual confirmation goes hand-in-hand with social recognition: he sees himself as a man, the group treats him as a man, and this public support reinforces a personal sense of his own manliness.[5]

In a sense, then, a rite of passage is a specialized form of ritual or tradition. The difference between a ritual and a rite of passage is their significance. Family rituals and traditions are celebrated for the sake of providing common experiences that help to give a family it's identity. They are symbolic of what already is, rather than of what is to be. They provide important bonding experiences and a sense of unity for all members of the family, but they don't mark a change in status for anyone.

A rite of passage, however, serves a unique purpose. It is a marker of sorts—marking a change in status. It marks what will now be, not just what is. The child is now recognized by others to be leaving one stage and entering the next stage of maturity.

CREATING RITES OF PASSAGE

We cannot change society. We cannot change how the rest of our community relates to our son. But as parents, we can choose to change the way we relate to our son. Therefore this chapter offers no single, dramatic event for you to mark your son's passage to adulthood. Instead, we want to give guidelines to help you commemorate and even initiate key points of maturity in your son's life. There is value in creating rites of passage for him as he matures and moves to adulthood.

These rites can be a natural outgrowth of the rituals and traditions that exist within our families. We don't have to do anything drastic. We don't have to go so far as to dig a pit for glowing embers of coal in the backyard, or send him out to the woods in a jockstrap to kill his first bear with a Ronco slingshot. But we do need to help him feel a sense of challenge and accomplishment that leads to treating him in a more adult way. Implementing some realistic family rites of passage will help your son's transition to manhood.

RITES OF SERVICE

This chapter offers six suggestions for developing rites of passage for your adolescent son. None is more important than suggestion No. 4: Connect the rite to some form of service.

Each adolescent playbook (beginning in chapter 7) includes one or more service projects for your son to undertake. (There are three possible projects in the early adolescent playbook, one in the middle-, and two in the late adolescent playbook.) These are optional plays; you may choose to do some and skip others. But their presence indicates the importance of service as an important kind of ritual.

As rites of passage, service projects can give your son vivid memories of helping others as he matures and of doing things of value. They will focus him away from himself and onto the needs of others. Perhaps most importantly, they will allow him to fulfill Christ's command to love his neighbor and make personal sacrifice. By so doing, his faith can grow.

Such projects also fulfill the second suggestion for any rite, that you make it a meaningful event. Remember, to make a lasting impression on your son, the rite should be something that will make a difference in his life. Service projects in which he interacts with others and offers a helping hand to those who need it, make that lasting impression.

Helping our sons develop service projects will require that we fathers look at ourselves. Do you have a servant heart that cares for and ministers to others? As a mark of Christlike maturity, this may be an area in your own life that needs some work. Maybe you can nurture it as you work alongside your son.

For each of the three stages of adolescence that are discussed in this book, we have made suggestions for some possible rites of passage that you can use with your son. They are shown in the three playbooks in chapters 7, 10, and 13. If you follow the suggestions that we give below, we can just about guarantee that it will make a positive difference in your relationship with your son and help him to mark his journey to manhood in a meaningful way.

There are six suggestions we want to give to you as you think about creating a rite of passage for your son: (1) keep it simple; (2) make it a meaningful event; (3) make it a time of affirmation; (4) try to connect it to some form of service; (5) mark it as a time for new responsibilities and privileges; and (6) recognize it as a change for the family, not just for your son.

1. Keep It Simple

A rite of passage does not need to be elaborate to be effective. Let's face it, most families would not even think about trying if the rite had to be complicated or outlandish. Dad, we know that you have no intention of asking your teenage son to put on a loincloth and paint himself with dyes made from the roots of various plants. A rite of passage needs to be something that all participants are willing to do, and for most men, that means it needs to be simple.

The important thing to remember is that there needs to be a concrete event that signals a new, more mature stage of growth. The ideas that are given in the three playbooks are very simple and easy, but they do take time and effort.

2. Make It a Meaningful Event

The significance of the rite of passage is not so much in what is done, but in why it is done. The rite is a symbolic event—it represents a change in status. Whatever the activity, it is vitally important that your son understands the meaning and significance of the event. That means you need to talk with him about it, dad. Let him know why it's important, both for him and for you. Rightly understood, you should both see it as an honor.

What you choose to use as rite of passage can make an impact on how meaningful it is. The more unusual or difficult the event, the more it will leave a lasting impression. You can have your son make peanut butter sandwiches for every family member, but more meaningful will be his giving a full weekend working at an inner-city mission. Be creative and take a risk! Choose something that will make a difference in his life, and then talk with him about the experience.

3. Make It a Time of Affirmation

Encouragement or criticism—which do you prefer? The ups and downs of everyday life can slide us toward focusing on what our children do wrong more than what they do right. But our children are a gift from God, uniquely created and of tremendous value. A rite of passage is a wonderful time to recognize and celebrate this fact.

Tell your son that you love him, honor him in front of the family and others, and help him to feel good about who God has made him to be. Make it a time of real blessing. Counselors and authors Gary Smalley and John Trent offer many suggestions in the book appropriately entitled *The Blessing*.[6]

4. Connect It to Some Form of Service

One of the marks of being Christlike is to develop a servant heart. As Jesus said, "The Son of Man did not come to be served, but to serve" (Matthew 20:28). A mark of maturity, spiritual or otherwise, is a concern for others and a desire to be of service to them.

As we help our sons grow to godly manhood, we can provide them with opportunities to cultivate this quality in their lives. A rite of passage that involves service to others can be a unique experience that makes a lasting impact. For this reason, we have included some possible rites of passage that involve service to others for each adolescent stage.

5. Mark It as a Time for New Responsibilities and Privileges

Responsibility and privilege are two sides of the same coin. Children often pout about the fact that they are unable to do what their older siblings get to do, and teens long for the day when they can "do whatever they want." Adults, on the other hand, can sometimes be heard to say that they long for the carefree days of childhood when they were not weighed down by responsibility. The truth is, privilege and responsibility go hand in hand. We do gain more privilege as we become adults, but we also gain more responsibility.

The tug-of-wars that parents experience with their teens as they move toward adulthood are often a result of this fact—teens focus on gaining privileges, while parents focus on the need for additional responsibility. Healthy development will include growing amounts of both privilege and responsibility. With each rite of passage, parents can negotiate with their son some new privileges that he can enjoy, and also the new responsibilities he must embrace.

6. *Recognize It as a Time of Change for the Family*

Throughout this book we will talk about your growing son and how rites of passage can help him to feel good about his emerging adulthood. However, the reality is that the family changes with your son, and the rites of passage signal a transition point for every family member, not just your son. As Edwin Friedman has noted,

> A family model of rites of passage creates a different perspective. When family systems concepts are applied to such . . . events, it becomes clear that, far from being an intermediary, it is the family itself that is going through the passage, rather than only some "identified" celebrant(s) and the family may actually go through more change than the focused member(s).[7]

The change in your son's status that comes with each new stage of adolescence needs to be more than just cosmetic. If we are going to help our sons grow to godly manhood, we need to pay more than lip service to making that happen. That means we will need make changes in our own behavior and attitudes as we relate to him in new, more adultlike ways.

Closing the Loop

There you have it. Some general suggestions for how you can create meaningful events in your son's life that will help him to sense his growing manhood. Are they really that important? We believe they are. So do Smalley and Trent:

> Many men who grew up with a hole in their hearts never emotionally grow out of childhood. In many ways, by missing out on the affirmation of a father or other significant male figure, they never "close the loop" on childhood and can remain emotional adolescents. . . . For those who have an older son at home, we have a special challenge and question for you. Have you helped close the loop on childhood for your son? Have you taken him to dinner, written him a letter, taken him for a long walk, given him a plaque, or in some other way communicated verbally that he's no longer just your child, but a man in your eyes?[8]

In each of the three sections on adolescence that follow, we will be providing you with some specific examples of family traditions and rites of passage that you can try with your son. All can be a part of what Smalley and Trent call "closing the loop," changing boys to men.

We have categorized these traditions and rites into five significant areas of your son's life: his family life, his social life, his spiritual life, his school life, and his interior life (how he feels about himself). Feel free to pick and choose a rite of passage that you believe will be meaningful to both you and your son. Actually doing one is more important than thinking about which one you should do. If you follow through, it *will* make a difference in helping your boy become a man.

PART TWO
CHARTING THE ADOLESCENT YEARS

Fathers, do not exasperate your children; instead, bring them up in the training and instruction of the Lord.

Ephesians 6:4

FIVE

MENTAL NOTES: AGES 10–13

I (Steve) have a love-hate relationship with my computer. I know, it's a machine that can't talk or go places with me. But it can help to make my life easier. (Notice I say *can* help.) When do I love my computer? I love it when it does what I want. Sometimes I can sit down and cruise through a variety of tasks without running into any trouble. All of the information I feed to it and the instructions I give are accepted with ease. I love it when we understand each other that way.

I hate my computer when it doesn't understand me and flashes error messages on the screen. It should understand what I mean—after all, my communication makes perfect sense to me. Our relationship would be a lot better if it would just take the information I give to it and interpret it in the way that I want. But it doesn't work that way.

I have had to learn that my computer processes information in a certain way. The problems come when I try to tell it to do things with commands or instructions that it doesn't understand. It amazes me how, as I learn more about the way my computer "thinks," the better we get along.

How does your young teenage son process information? Dads often make the mistake of assuming that their children think about life and relationships in the same way that we do. They don't. Our kids are not adults. When we treat them as if they can understand things in the same way that adults can, we set ourselves up for misunderstandings and frustrations.

We will begin with what many experts classify as the early adolescent boy. He is age ten through thirteen and on the verge of major changes. (Yes, we're going to include the ten- , eleven- , and twelve-year-old in the young teen category, for the changes of early adolescence often begin before the magic age of thirteen.) His mind, his body, and his relationships will soon transform, and growth—and confusion—will result. As a father, you need to understand and recognize these changes as they appear.

What goes on in the mind of a ten- to thirteen-year-old boy? How does he look at his world and the people in it? How does he think about God and the Christian life? How does he see his family? No doubt his beliefs, attitudes, and values—those things that are important to him—are being shaped. We fathers need to "get inside his head" and understand life from his point of view if we want to avoid "error messages" in our relationship with him.

HIS MENTAL FRAMEWORK

What do we know about the thinking of young boys who are on the brink of adolescence? Research suggests that the typical mental framework of children in this age range includes: (1) an emphasis on here-and-now experience, (2) a focus on personal experience as reality, (3) a tendency toward sequential thinking (what happened) rather than analytical thinking (what it meant), and (4) a willingness to accept things at face value. Let's consider how each of these four areas affects the thinking of the early adolescent.

An Emphasis on Present Experience

The most important day in the life of an early adolescent is today. Little thought is given to what has already happened, and not much more thought is given to what is going to happen. Take baseball, for example.

In the Denver suburb where I (Chap) live, youth baseball begins the first week of March and runs through the summer. For the past four years my son Chappie has been on the same team, with the same coach. Mrs. Taylor (not her real name) is the mom of two of the boys on the team, and she does a great job teaching not only baseball, but also caring for each boy as a unique individual. She does at times, however, fail to recognize how ten- to thirteen-year-old boys think. In the heat of coaching, she sometimes fails to recognize the way the boys see life in the here-and-now.

After each game, win or lose, Chappie's coach has this ritual: she will systematically go through most every play, good and bad. Mrs.

Taylor explains what they had done well, and talks about what they needed to work on. The parents typically stand around and nod, trusting that this information was seeping into the heads of the boys.

During those talks, Mrs. Taylor failed to remember that at this stage of development, almost anything other than hands-on input, in this case during practice sessions, would quickly be forgotten, if understood at all. By the time the next game had rolled around, the information from her speech would be long gone. Early adolescents live in the concrete world of the present.

Dick kept hoping that Jason, his eleven-year-old son, would start taking his studies at school more seriously. Like most boys his age, Jason was not particularly fond of school. He would much rather be roller-blading with his friends or watching television. Unfortunately, school work did not come easily to Jason, and he was in danger of failing a couple of classes.

Dick decided that he would reward Jason with a trip to Disney World at the end of the school year if Jason could get his grades up. Jason was excited about the deal, but he didn't follow through on working harder.

Dick was frustrated and confused. *Man, I can't think of a bigger reward than this,* he thought to himself. *What's it going to take to light a fire under him?*

Dick made the mistake of promising something that was too far off in the distance. His intentions were good, but he needed to understand that eleven-year-old boys live in the present, not the future. They seldom have the patience to wait for things they want. Why put off pleasure today for something that seems so far off? (Many adults never learn how to get past this kind of thinking, either.)

Once Dick realized his mistake, he set up very short-term, immediate rewards for Jason. Meeting daily and weekly goals paid off in small but meaningful ways—a trip to Dairy Queen, renting a special video movie, going to a game with dad, etc. Gradually Jason's grades began to creep up, and by the end of the school year, both Dick and Jason were happy with the progress that had been made.

Adults often spend time longing for the past or living for the future. Young adolescent boys do not. While they remember the past and look forward to things in the future, they live in the present.

The Reality of Personal Experience

The thinking of early adolescence is still rather childlike, in spite of a growing exposure to a complex world. Whether age ten or twelve, a boy during early adolescence has not yet acquired the ability to think in the abstract. (By age thirteen he is just beginning to think abstractly.) His thinking and problem-solving involve objects, relationships, or situations with which he can identify personally.

Young children have a difficult time understanding that a person can be more than one thing at a time. The idea that dad can be a dad, a banker, and a son all at the same time is hard to comprehend. As children grow, however, they gain the ability to recognize the reality that a person can be many things simultaneously. They gain experience in having to see their dad in various roles, and come to understand that being one thing does not mean you can't be something else.

At twelve years of age, Ryan has no problem understanding that I (Steve) am his dad and a college teacher at the same time. He has visited my college classes, and he has experienced me in both roles. However, he has a more difficult time seeing me as a child. While he accepts the fact that I once was one, that is ancient history and he has no experience with my childhood. Ryan's brother, Trevor, is age sixteen. Those four additional years of maturity give him the ability to imagine what my childhood must have been like much better than Ryan. While he has no experience with his dad as a child, he has gained the ability to think about that possibility.

Thinking in Sequence

Life for a young adolescent consists of a series of events. If you ask a son at this age to think about the "big picture" of his experiences and to tell you the lessons from them, expect a bleak stare and a simple "I don't know, Dad." His thinking is less analytical, more sequential.

I saw this recently after our family finished watching the movie "Cool Runnings"—the story of the first Jamaican bobsled team. When Ryan talked about that movie, he usually gave a play-by-play account of the story. He provided an accurate description of what happens. First this happens, then this, then this, and on and on until the whole story is told (if you can stand to listen that long).

On the other hand, sixteen-year-old Trevor always included the overall theme of the story. He described how a group of Jamaican athletes worked to overcome the odds in reaching the Olympics, persevering in the face of adversity. He has a better sense of the theme of the movie, not just the sequence of events that make it up.

Think of a movie film on a reel. Early adolescents think about their life and relationships as if the film were rolling, frame by frame. As each frame is viewed, eventually they blend together to tell a story. In contrast, older teens have gained the ability to take the film off the reel and turn it sideways. This gives them the opportunity to look at many frames at the same time in order to discover the overall themes and lessons. Young adolescent boys have a difficult time turning the film.

At times, listening to a detailed, play-by-play account of anything by an early adolescent can lead to impatience. One of the current hot topics among Ryan's friends is the world of video and computer games. Parents in the next room and teachers listening as seventh graders return from recess probably hear the same thing: "Can I borrow your Game Boy?" "Did you get to the next level of Mario Brothers?" Listening to a fifteen-minute description of a computer or video game can be a tough assignment, especially when you have no idea who X-men are or what a Sonic Hedgehog is. Trevor sometimes interrupts Ryan and tells him to get to the point—and that's exactly what Ryan thinks he is doing. He is a typical twelve-year-old.

Accepting Things at Face Value

For the most part, early adolescent boys still accept what their parents have to say as being truth. They have not yet reached the point where parental wisdom is something to be questioned.

A friend was lamenting the changes that adolescence brings for parents by describing an encounter he had had with his two boys while driving across Pennsylvania. Crossing over a fairly substantial river, his ten-year-old asked, "Daddy, how deep is that water?" Without pausing, he gave a standard, parental answer he had gotten used to delivering over the years, "Twelve feet."

Before Johnny, age ten, could respond with even an "ooh" or an "ahh," clearly impressed by the immense wisdom of his father, his fourteen-year-old brother shot back, *"What? There's no way it is only twelve feet deep, Dad! Look at the way the water looks like it's standing still. My teacher says that means it is very, very deep. And it is a lot deeper in the middle. I don't think you're right about this one, dad. What I think is . . ."* And on and on it went. Finally this father said to his ten-year-old, "Don't listen to your brother. It's twelve feet deep," and turned on the radio.

If you don't know it yet, dad, this is your last major chance to give your son instruction that will be accepted in childlike innocence. As your son progresses through this stage, you will notice an increasing reluctance to accept things just because you say them.

How He Views His World

So what does all this mean for your growing son? It means he will have a distinct view of himself, his parents, and his Christian faith. Let's take a look at how his thinking affects those three areas.

Viewing Himself

In general, the ten- to thirteen-year-old boy accepts his own self-opinion at face value. He has gained the ability to think of personal qualities that he has, for instance, good in math, kind to other people, and outgoing. That does not mean that he necessarily likes who he is. But liked or not, that's just the way things are. He also believes that those are the qualities that others see in him.

An early adolescent has a sense of how well he measures up to his peers in a variety of areas, such as intelligence, athletic ability, and his ability to make and keep friends. His evaluation of where he stands in each of these areas is based on his experience. This can create a mixed bag when it comes to self-esteem, especially if he sees himself as very competent in one area and incompetent in another. But however he sees it, he accepts his opinion as fact.

Viewing His Parents

Early adolescents are generally still open to instruction and accept what parents have to say as the way things are. Parents are assumed to know what they are talking about. (Enjoy it while it lasts.) This is a prime time for parental teaching.

As early adolescents are beginning to think of life and relationships in new ways, they are like young players on an athletic team. When I (Steve) played football in high school, I still remember coming into fall practice as a green freshman. There was a lot to learn, and I was anxious to please my coach. I listened intently to what he had to say, and trusted that he knew what he was talking about. But some of the "veteran" players (mostly seniors) seemed to ignore what the coach had to say. They even complained that he didn't know what he was doing. They felt free to point out his "mistakes," but never to his face.

Our young sons are like green freshman in the game of adolescence. They respect what we have to say and generally accept our statements as true. They think we know what we're talking about, and they usually take what we have to say at face value. It's a great time for giving them a good background in the rules of the game and the skills

U nderstanding your son may seem difficult due to different kinds of thinking between a father and son. Yet as you look at this chapter and the mental notes for the mid- and late adolescent (chapters 8 and 11), keep in mind that a strong relationship can often act as a bridge over the swirling waters of misunderstanding during the teen years.

Research in the area of father-son relationships cite three main factors in achieving a healthy and mutually satisfying relationship; these can give you a strong chance of raising a healthy son.

First, both the fathers and sons in such relationships say they have a warm relationship. As nebulous as this may sound, it has been proven time and again to be the single most important predictor of relational satisfaction and intimacy. If either a son or a father believes that the other person is cold in relation to him, there will be a significant block in their communication and relationship, thus hindering a father's ability to nurture and influence his son through adolescence.

Second, the father's problem-solving ability and communication skills, as well as his ability to pass that on to his son, can benefit the relationship. This has a wide range of applications, but the father who can help his son to think strategically and critically when making decisions, who knows how to listen and interact, who can communicate feelings as well as convictions, as well as teach a son how to factor in consequences when making choices, is well on the road to helping his son become a healthy man of God.

Third, a mutual trust exists. Most parents look at this as a one-way proposition, ignoring whether their son is trustworthy. But healthy relationships have two-way trust. The trust between you and your son should be mutual, and an issue the two of you discuss and evaluate from time to time.

Here are several questions you can ask yourself to measure the trust level between your son and you: Can your son trust you to listen to him when circumstances look bad? Can he trust you to take him at his word, even when you don't want to? Does your son trust that you care more about him than how well he achieves in sports, activities, or even grades? Does he believe that you like him as he is, and that he can open himself up to you without fear of condemnation or ridicule?

they will need to succeed. Make the most of it, though. Their freshman enthusiasm won't last forever.

Viewing the Christian Faith

For the most part, a young boy's religious values and understanding are the result of his parent's faith. That is not to say that his Christian faith is not real, but a child does not yet possess the ability to think deeply about why he believes as he does. While he can describe basic reasons for his faith, he has a hard time thinking about why those reasons are true. For example, he may be able to say that the Bible is God's Word to us. But if you ask him how he knows that the Bible is God's Word, the average early adolescent boy will be at a loss to give you any kind of answer.

The faith of most young boys is strongly connected to the faith of their parents. If religion is very important to the parents, then religion will be felt as very important to the child. An interesting finding in one study was that the amount of "God-talk" in the home is a crucial factor in passing the Christian faith on to our children, and that it is particularly important for dads to participate in this process.[1] In fact, the significance of fathers as compared with mothers grows in a number of areas as boys progress through adolescence.

It is encouraging that there is a relationship between how important a young boy reports religion to be in his life and a number of positive characteristics. Boys who say that religion is important to them are more likely to have high self-esteem, to show helping behaviors and concern for others, and to refrain from using drugs and alcohol.[2]

LIKE FATHER, LIKE SON?

You may be scratching your head by now, wondering what's so unique about these characteristics. As adults, we often think and make decisions the same way. After all, we were young adolescents once, and we can still use the thinking patterns we used then. But we have also grown past those patterns, and we often lose sight of the fact that young teens have not yet gained the ability to think in more sophisticated ways.

We think in the here-and-now, but we also can effectively think in future terms and plan for what might be. Remember Dick, convinced that rewarding his son with an eventual trip to Disney World would be a powerful motivator? His effort didn't register with Jason, because young boys only know what it's like to live life in the present.

Like our early adolescent sons, we use our experiences to help us understand life and make decisions; but unlike our sons we also can think and make decisions based on what could be and on other people's experiences. We have an easier time understanding that not everyone sees things our way, and we can accept that fact more readily than a young adolescent.

We, too, can think in a straight line. We are able to tell stories point by point, but we can also pull out the overall gist or meaning of an event.

We often take things at face value, but we can also ask questions that challenge.

When we attempt to teach our sons by communicating with them in ways that are beyond their mental abilities, we confuse them. While your son might shake his head and say he understands, don't count on it. If you want to relate well with your son, match your thinking and communication to his level.

One of the best ways to know whether your son is learning what you want is to ask for feedback. As you talk with him about life, relationships, or the Christian faith, ask him questions to find out what he already knows. Listen for the way he looks at these issues. Then, as you try to instruct him by sharing new information and perspectives, ask him to tell you what he thinks you are saying. Think of examples he can identify with, and keep at it until you are sure he understands. Don't just assume he knows what you mean. It's worth the time and effort.

SIX

PARENTS, PEERS, AND (GULP!) PUBERTY

W hen your son hits about eleven years old, say good-bye to your little boy, dad. While he may still look, talk, think, and act like a little boy, that will not last much longer. Big changes are just around the bend. People who work with kids this age see it all the time. Last spring we visited with Ryan's sixth-grade teacher. The conversation got around to discussing the typical developmental changes that begin to take place in early adolescence. "A lot of parents don't really see it coming," she began. "I've found that the best way to bring it to their attention is to say, 'Take your family pictures this year, because by next year they won't look like innocent kids anymore.'" She's right.

Not only will your son lose his "little boyness" within the next year or two, but you will not see him as often either. Early adolescence marks a major shift from parents to peers. His social world is expanding. And leading the charge to social change is that blessing and curse of boys growing into men—puberty.

HERE COME THE HORMONES!

As we noted in the previous chapter, early adolescence is a relatively peaceful time where relationships with parents are still close. That childlike innocence we have known for the past ten years has not yet disappeared. But at some point during this stage, that will begin to change. As one parent put it, "Eleven year olds are an accident waiting to happen." Most of the change will be created when the rush of hormones hits to usher in puberty.

Over the years we have asked both students and adults, "How many of you would like to return to junior high school, those early days of puberty?" If memory serves us right, no one has ever raised his hand; that's just not a time of life to which people would like to return. Clearly puberty brings significant physical and emotional changes, and all the confusion that goes with them. One man likened puberty to hitting his head against the wall—it hurts so bad, but it feels so good when it's over.

Although many young boys handle the changes that puberty brings with relative ease, it can also change some pretty nice kids into moody monsters. For every young adolescent, there is some degree of confusion, awkwardness, and self-consciousness that accompanies the onset of puberty. Oversized feet, a new crop of body hair, wet dreams—these and many other changes pose a real challenge as they adapt to their new physical and social worlds.

Early Puberty

The powerful effects of this process have been demonstrated in the research on early versus late puberty. The onset of puberty, especially if you are an early or late maturer, has been shown to impact on body image, moods and emotions, relationships with parents, and relationships with peers.

Just how does the timing of puberty effect development? In general, early puberty is more often a positive experience for boys than late puberty. The benefits of puberty tend to begin in sixth-grade, but the full impact of maturing early is more often felt in seventh and eighth grade, as physical changes collide head-on with social changes. Specifically, the advantages of developing early tend to include:

- greater satisfaction with how he looks and with life in general
- an increase in size and muscle, a welcome change that often signifies being athletic and strong
- more positive feelings about himself
- higher levels of self-confidence
- greater popularity with peers
- an advantage in gaining leadership positions, both in formal settings (athletic teams, school offices) and informal ones (standing within the peer group)

The only real disadvantage of developing early for a boy seems to be that he may have trouble living up to the expectations of his parents or other adults. Parents and teachers may expect him to act his appearance, not his age.

Late Puberty

On the other hand, developing late is associated with a number of disadvantages. Boys who mature late are at the tail end of their peer group. In general, girls begin puberty before most boys, and early maturing boys come next. So while the rest of their peers are now looking more adultlike, late-maturing boys are still small and boyish-looking. Their behavior is often a reflection of their looks—they act more childish than their maturing peers. They long for the day when they will change in appearance. As a result, they often find themselves having to live with:

- lower self-esteem
- higher levels of insecurity
- feelings of inferiority and rejection
- name-calling and teasing (squirt, wimp, or worse)[1]

Researchers have found that many of the negative effects of puberty, especially for these boys who mature late, can be softened by strong, supportive relationships with family and friends. The effects of puberty can be felt for a long time, so it is important that we give this support to our sons. In looking back on his early adolescence, one twelfth grade boy reflected, "My worst time was seventh to ninth grade. I had a lot of growing up to do, and I still have a lot more to do. High school was not the sweet sixteen time everyone said it would be. What would have helped me is more emotional support in grades seven through nine."[2]

Keep in mind as we look at the relationships an early adolescent has with his family and peers that puberty is powerful. We need to avoid the mistake of assuming that our son is in complete control of all his emotions and reactions. Hormones speak loudly, and while we cannot change when and how they speak, we can help our sons to understand what they are saying.

Relationships with Family

If you have a son between ten and thirteen, just at the verge of change but not fully in the grasp of puberty, you may want to keep things right there. Steve's pastor has a twelve-year-old son, Nathan.

PARENTS, PEERS, AND (GULP!) PUBERTY

Concerning their relationship, the pastor concluded, "I'd like to just freeze time right now. I enjoy him so much—better than any other time of his life. We're having a great time together." I know what he means. I don't really long for the days of changing Ryan's diapers, patting in order to get a burp, or reading a favorite Sesame Street book for the thousandth time. But the fun we have together now is very satisfying.

I realize that not all dads are experiencing that kind of time together and enjoyment of their ten- or thirteen-year-old son. The warmth and love of our relationship has been cultivated over the years. There is reciprocal influence in any relationship—how I relate to my son affects our relationship, and the same is true of him. Relationships are not a one-way street. Some children are easier to deal with than others. It's easy to be warm and loving with your son if he responds with warmth and love.

Previous patterns of interaction set the stage for what your relationship with your son will look like during this period of his life. If those patterns have been healthy, you can expect that to continue during this time. A young adolescent boy still feels close to his parents and sees them as a major source of support. While he enjoys spending time with friends, his relationships with his parents are still the most important relationships in his life.

Studies have found some interesting differences in how early adolescents view their parents. Boys tend to rate mothers and fathers equally well as companions, but fathers are routinely viewed as the enforcer of family rules and values. A child begins to feel that he may be able to get away with more when dealing with mom rather than dad. As he moves closer to puberty, a boy may even start to get mouthy with mom in a way that he wouldn't dare try with dad. But overall, the decline in parental power is pretty minimal at this stage—at least compared to middle and late adolescence.

When teens are asked about who they can count on for emotional and social support, moms win. Dads are seen as providing significantly less support than mom (though they come out better than teachers). At the same time, boys see dads as being not only more willing, but also more excited, about letting them grow up.[3] Moms are less willing to let their little boy start his journey to manhood.

Remember that puberty is rearing its head for most boys by the end of this stage. While boys vary in how they handle puberty, one thing is for sure—your son will never be your little boy again. It does not matter if you do not want them to grow up. You had better get ready to relate with them in new ways.

The feelings of affection that can be so strong at the beginning of early adolescence are now more shaky. Parents and sons both report that these feelings for each other decline from the sixth to the eighth grade. It is encouraging, however, that the decline is from very positive to less positive—not to negative.[4]

Puberty also brings less time at home. Your growing son will now want to spend more time with his friends, and he is also likely to become more involved with school or community activities.

RELATIONSHIPS WITH PEERS

A popular TV show of the late eighties followed a boy growing up, leaving elementary school for junior high. Viewers followed Kevin Arnold during what were called "The Wonder Years." That's a good way to describe the changes and adventure of early adolescence. The show was so successful that it continued to follow Kevin and his friends through high school. But the true wonder years were his late elementary and early junior high experiences.

Kevin had two close friends, Paul and Winnie; later Winnie became his girlfriend. The theme music for the show was the Beatles' tune, "With a Little Help from My Friends," and Kevin's triumphs and setbacks with his friends were chronicled weekly. The show's producers were right about that element of early adolescence: friends play a significant role in a boy's life during these years.

During those wonder years, your children will develop new friendships, and gradually they will spend more time with friends than previously. As parents, we wonder about the influence of those friends. The good news is that the quality of friends your son selects generally is not much of a problem in early adolescence. Get-togethers with friends who do not live in the neighborhood or nearby still depend on parental cooperation (although you can quickly start to feel like a chauffeur). Interactions with friends can still be controlled and regulated by parents as they see fit.

As your son approaches middle adolescence, however, be aware that controlling his interactions will become more difficult. You will be forced to trust your son because you have no other choice. What he does with the time that he spends with friends away from your home will be his choice, and his responsibility. You hope that the training and values you have tried to instill in him will see him through. The early adolescent playbook presented in chapter 7 will give helpful guidelines for establishing such training and worthwhile traditions early in his adolescent years.

Finding Friends

Who do young adolescent boys choose as friends? For the most part, they choose friends who are their same age and have similar interests to their own. They also tend to associate with boys who come from families that have similar values to their own. Groups of friends seem to form where there are similar involvements and behaviors at school as well. Students who earn good grades, who take their homework seriously, and who are involved in extracurricular activities associate with others who do the same. Unfortunately, the reverse is also true.

In addition to the above similarities, there is one other obvious similarity—boys at this age pick boys as friends. There is very little mixing of the sexes when it comes to friends. The small, same-sex cliques that are formed will eventually make forays into opposite-sex interactions as they move toward the end of this stage and encounter puberty. When boys get together, they often interact with each other in ways that increase their immaturity—they get to a point where their behavior can only be described as "squirrelly." Their silliness may reach a point where a parent needs to step in and settle them down, but they know how to have fun with each other.

Boys value having a number of friends that they can call or spend time with. That way, if some are busy or unavailable, there is always someone else to connect with. This desire for a large number of friends is different than that for girls. Girls at this age prefer to have one best friend or a small circle of close friends. Their friendships tend to be deeper and more personal than those of boys.

Interest in Girls

Since girls reach puberty first, their interest in boys is often met with indifference. Boys are still involved in life as a child. In contrast, many sixth-grade girls are already moving through puberty and are ready to socialize with boys; most boys have not reached that point. As one girl put it, "Girls think about boys more than boys think about girls." The animosity that boys have held for girls in elementary school is softening, however. I recently asked Ryan if he was interested in girls yet, or just what he thought of them. He replied, "Well, dad, they don't have cooties anymore. I guess they're just people. But I'd rather play with my friends." His older brother informed him that those days are numbered.

Once boys begin to mature, they quickly catch up in opposite-sex interest. The boys who hit puberty early are usually the pioneers in

DADS HAVE FEELINGS, TOO

M ost dads begin to have similar feelings as their sons change socially, and understanding those emotions is just as important as understanding your son. As men, we need to admit that we don't always have our act together, and there are times when our emotions get the best of us.

Not all of these emotions will arrive during this stage of early adolescent growth, but chances are good that they will surface within the next few years. The six emotions listed are based on the work of Bruce Baldwin.[5]

1. *Pure fear.* While the social world of the early adolescent is rather small at first, it gradually expands to include more people and more time away from home. The world is a more dangerous place today than it was a generation ago, and parents often fear for the physical and emotional safety of their growing child. There are plenty of things to be afraid of today—violence, drugs, drunk drivers, peer pressure, immoral media—the list could go on. It does not help that their movement into this more dangerous world happens at about the same time that they become more private about what is going on in their life. The fear factor kicks into action.

2. A *sense of helplessness.* Helplessness is a difficult feeling for us men to handle—we want to be able to control life. But there will be times when, as a dad, you can do nothing but stand back and watch the pain and turmoil that your young son will experience at times. Even when you try to offer support, your son's own suspicion or budding need for independence may cause him to push you away—to shut you out.

   We cannot always rush in and rescue our son from the cruelties of other teens or the consequences of their own actions. Life can be a hard teacher. But you can help your son, as later chapters will show (see especially the playbooks).

3. *Inadequacy.* It would be good if we always knew what we are doing as a parent. We don't. Living with a teenager will at least occasionally highlight that fact, and feelings of inadequacy are sure to follow. When that happens, it is important to remember that it's OK to feel them. We can learn from our mistakes and press on in our attempt to be the best dad we can be.[6]

4. *Frustration and anger.* It is inevitable that some of the behaviors that accompany growing up will frustrate you and trigger your anger. Our sons' push for independence will show up in resistance, the testing of limits, and emotional swings. Frustration and anger will be normal, and perhaps frequent, reactions. For the sake of our sons, we need to learn to resolve that anger in appropriate ways.

5. *A growing awareness of loss.* We don't always like to admit it, but our sons are growing up. We already feel some loss as they are involved more and more in a life away from home. We are forced to realize that in just a few short years they will be going into the real world and lost to our families forever (at least in a formative, growing kind of way). The positive side of this awareness is that it motivates us to be an active part of their life now, before we lose the chance.

6. *Excitement.* Negative emotions are a natural part of parenting a growing adolescent. But in healthy families there are lots of positive emotions, too. As much as we are not looking forward to the day when our boys will no longer live at home, there are also times when we get excited about their growth toward manhood. Healthy father-son relationships will have these moments of excitement, not because we are anxious to see them go, but because we look forward to seeing them become their own person.

exploring social relations with girls. They're willing to talk with girls and to be seen talking with them (though often boys feel safer talking via phone or alone after school). They may experiment with having longer conversations on the phone or actually having a girlfriend (defined as someone you like and spend time talking with in the hall at school). Some boys will even start to date and try out some displays of affection. Young adolescents who look like teenagers seem to want to act like them as well.

Electronic Friends

Next to the amount of time that they spend with friends, early adolescent boys spend a lot of time watching television and playing with electronic technology. One of the significant changes for boys at this stage in recent years has been the growing preoccupation with computer/ video games. It seems as if everyone has access to Super Nintendo®, Sega Genesis®, Game Gear®, or any number of other systems. And parents are only too aware of the expense involved in outfitting their children with the latest system, not to mention the price of the computer programs or game cartridges. Hundreds of dollars worth of equipment and games now sit neglected in closets across the country, as the game manufacturers update the system and require would-be video wizards to get the latest gear.

And the computer game phenomenon can make boyhood friendships superficial at times. Recently, Robbie had a friend over to spend the night. The two spent several hours in the basement, playing games almost nonstop. For awhile, they played against each other. But soon, they decided to separate, and one hit the computer while another stayed with Sega. A half hour or so later they switched. They were together for the evening, but mentally, and socially, they were worlds apart.

How a Father Can Help

So what does all of this mean for you, dad? First, spend time with your son! Relationships are forged in the context of time. You cannot build a strong relationship without spending quantity, not just quality, time together. That is a principle that holds for all relationships—with your God, your spouse, and your children.

As our sons move through this stage and on into their teenage years, spending time with them becomes more of a problem. In fact, finding them becomes more of a problem. So make the most of your opportunities to do things together with your son. Plant warm memories of special times together in his mind.

Second, support his involvement in various activities by your attendance. Go to his concerts, his games, his school plays, his science fairs. Your support will give him a sense of security and competence. He may not thank you for going, but you can be sure that he will remember your tangible expression of love and support well into his adult life. I (Steve) grew up with a much stronger interest in sports than in music. I participated in band and choir when I was growing up, but my real love was (and still is) sports. I confess that it is much easier for me to get excited about going to my sons' sporting activities than their music concerts. But the fact that they are playing in that concert is important to me, and I never regret going.

Be an encourager more than an enforcer. The fact that many early adolescent boys see mom as the clear winner when it comes to emotional support is a powerful challenge for us dads. Many dads also make the mistake of paying the most attention to their sons when they fail to "toe the mark," and their interactions end up centering on enforcing the house rules. Out of love for our sons, we may also try to help them in their quest for maturity by offering "suggestions" and "constructive criticism."

Unfortunately, our sons may interpret our efforts as indicators that they are not measuring up to our expectations. Our correction and criticism will be accepted more enthusiastically if it is sprinkled rather than poured. What needs to be poured is the message that our sons are loved and accepted unconditionally, and that we will stand by them through their struggles, a source of security.

Third, talk with your son about what is ahead in his life while he is still wide open to your instruction. Talk with him about the changes he can expect when puberty arrives. Talk with him about your hopes and dreams for his teenage years. Talk with him about relationships with friends and girls. Just talk to him. This may not seem like a very practical suggestion given what we said about how boys think at this age. Talking about the future will not have an immediate impact. But as your son begins to experience some of the things you can talk about, he may remember his talks with you and be more open to further discussion.

All in all, our early adolescent sons are gradually moving toward what is reported by many as one of the most difficult stages in life. As they do, our boys need our time and strong support, even though our sons are making choices that take them away from home more and more. Remember, too, that your son also needs his friends, for they provide him with the support that he needs when he is away from home.

SEVEN
THE EARLY ADOLESCENT PLAYBOOK

Two fathers, two sons. Both boys were entering the mine field of adolescence. Both enjoyed their dads, and liked spending time with them, doing what they liked to do, sports, camping—the usual.

Bruce's son, Don, was seen by his dad as a "chip off the old block." Bruce knew that Don could be a good athlete, if he would work hard and apply himself. So, in the name of love, Bruce encouraged Don to go after several sports. When Don seemed to his father to be lazy, or not "into" the sport, Bruce worked overtime to help his son work at it, to improve by practice. He wanted Don to realize how "anything of value and of excellence takes work, effort, and focused attention," as he told his son.

Randy's son, Jared, was a relatively quiet kid as he entered adolescence. Randy loved spending time focused on sports and activities with Jared, but during the teen years Jared preferred taking walks with his dad or playing Frisbee at the beach to attending a baseball game or having his dad coach one of his teams. So Randy accepted Jared's desires and loved his son as he was. Jared was a gifted athlete and practiced some, yet Randy determined to let Jared choose his own sport, in his own time.

Don, wanting primarily to please his dad, went on to become a fairly good basketball player at a small Christian high school. The years were bittersweet, however, for even as Don moved into a starting role, culminating years of work and dedication, he was harboring mixed feelings of frustration, insecurity, and resentment, most of which were secretly directed at his father. He wanted to succeed in sports, but for all the wrong reasons. In contrast to this, as Jared grew, Randy's tenderness and acceptance of Jared to pursue his own dreams and goals freed him up to move through adolescence with one less pressure than most kids face—the pressure to perform for Dad.

Jared was convinced that his father was for him, no matter what activities he participated in, or even how well he did. Interestingly enough, Jared went on to stand out as a major college shortstop, who was marked by an ability to excel under pressure, because he was able to play a sport—as novel as it may sound—for fun!

The last two chapters have given you some handles on what happens during this first step into adolescence. But knowing about what an early adolescent faces and feeling prepared to handle it are two very different issues. For many parents, especially fathers, the advent of adolescence is often a time of foreboding. It has been compared to a fast approaching spring storm—you know something powerful is in the works, but you are not sure just how severe it's going to be. To many parents, this is the time which marks the arrival of those "dreaded teenage years!"

If you are just entering this stage of life, especially with your first child, you know how ominous this transition can seem. Your son has just left the carefree time of being a seven- to ten-year-old, a period that most boys are fairly comfortable with. Toward the end of that period he had begun to display an occasional flash of adult humor and timing, and is sometimes the most rational member during family discussions. Children this age are responsive, articulate, and relationally freed up to be themselves with few social worries. They are a joy to spend time with, to talk to, and to play with. They are fun![1]

Now, though, you may be tempted to shout, "What happened to my little boy! Where did he go?"

Yes, this phenomenon called adolescence disrupts family dynamics that once felt relatively stable. But what most parents often fail to recognize is that this time of life is often unsettling and can even be incredibly difficult for the child himself.

A WHOLE NEW WORLD

Though he may act differently, your son is not gone. The changes and moods that accompany adolescence do not mean that he has left you, but rather that he is in process—an exciting, frightening, lonely, busy, fulfilling process that will ultimately lead him to manhood. Adolescence is a time of joy, celebration, and anticipation more than it is a time of foreboding and conflict. Trust that the early years of loving, correcting, and training your son are not tossed aside as he enters adolescence. Though there may be trials and turmoil along the way, for a great many families these years of transition only confirm the wonder of the man before you.

As your son enters this first phase of the adolescent process, early adolescence, he enters an exciting stage of observation. The world of a ten- to thirteen-year-old boy is full of fresh, new possibilities and perspectives. Girls take on a new meaning, achievement in activities, especially sports, becomes a more significant factor, and friends become emotionally preeminent. This time of observation, of once again trying to make sense out of family and friends and girls and faith, can be very frightening, especially if his parents are as thrown off as he is, and even more so if it's his dad! But he needs you to not only understand what he is going through; he needs your help in making the transition meaningful.

This book is intended to provide you with some tools and ideas to help you not only cope with adolescence, but enjoy the years, as Randy did with his son, Don. Just as a covered porch offers a sense of security during a storm, enabling a storm to be an experience filled with wonder and beauty, the suggestions we offer can make these days the highlight of the parenting years.

Adolescence does not need to be a time for fear and loathing. It can be an adventure of celebration as your son moves from childhood to becoming a man.

Rites, Ritual, and Ceremony

In chapter 4 we called for observing important events with ritual and creating memories through family traditions. Yet when it comes to such observances, most of us fear being labeled "old-fashioned" and "out of touch"; most fathers, concerned with time or money (and sometimes both), accept the maxim of a busy society that proclaims "The one with the most toys wins!" And so we let many opportunities to establish or continue family traditions pass by us.

Family vacation? "Can't go. Billy has football practice."

Birthday dinner? "Sorry, going to the mall."

Take a walk? Ride a bike? "Would if I could, son. But got no time; gotta keep moving!"

But ritual is important, even necessary, for making boys into men. As author Tony Campolo states,

> Those families that have a great deal of ritual are usually the ones that are the most solid and secure. They seem better able to impart to their children the values and truths which they believe to be of ultimate significance. Ritualistic families have propor-

tionately fewer juvenile delinquents, and their children are psychologically more healthy. Rituals are good for families, and instituting rituals makes family life more fun for everyone.[2]

As we mentioned in chapter 4, the main difference between a ritual and a rite of passage is that a rite is a specific type of ritual. It is ceremony in which a behavior is elevated above normal familial activity; it is a ritual as well—regular, expected, and anticipated.

The main feature that makes a rite of passage distinctive is that the behavior is understood for its significance as a marker of transition from one stage of adolescence to another. There must be an accompanying statement, usually verbal, ensuring that the entire family understands its meaning as a transitional marker. It is not something a dad does with or for his son that marks a rite of passage. Rather, it is a shared experience where both the son and other family members recognize that a shift has occurred, however minor.

The focus of this book is to help parents, especially fathers, create an environment whereby their sons become the men God has called them to be. In order to become that man, our sons need more than just family devotions and a few memory verses. A godly man is a man who has a healthy sense of self, a willingness to cooperate, who can make decisions recognizing and taking account of possible consequences. A man of God is more than a person who is a committed churchgoer and Sunday school teacher; he is a well-rounded leader in the world. "You are the light of the world," Jesus said to His disciples, and His declaration fits His disciples today. A light is a beacon of maturity, honesty, integrity, and hope. As fathers we are called to bring our sons to fullness in the whole package of manhood, not just in his faith.

The rites and rituals that follow are tools to enable you to help your son take those crucial beginning steps toward maturity in every area of his life. The five areas where your son lives provide the framework for these suggestions. They are not exhaustive, nor right for everyone. It is not necessary to try to do them all, or even most, and there is no "correct" or "best" suggestions. They can be, however, a helpful starting point in determining which rites and rituals you choose in caring for your son during this impressionable time.

Here is a playbook with several possible plays for the five situations our sons will find themselves in during early adolescence (and continuing throughout their teens). These "plays" are particularly suited for boys ages ten to thirteen.

FAMILY PLAYS

1. *Commit to regular "dates," preferably monthly.* Such events tell your son that he is important enough to be placed on your calendar. Most of us keep schedules that are very busy. It says a lot to your son when he knows that he is valued in a way that gives him a special place in that daily organizer you keep. The goal is to go one-on-one, with no distractions to get in the way.

You can organize and structure these times in several ways so they can take on ritualistic significance, and ultimately can be made into a rite of passage. Here are three approaches:

- **a.** Every other month, for fun and adventure. This can be negotiated, or sometimes you can surprise each other. You may end up at the park, the bowling alley, a ballgame, a movie, a restaurant, or any number of other places.
- **b.** Every other month, for communication and problem-solving. You don't need a date for this, but it is a tremendous gift for your son to know that every two months you will go out to lunch or dinner just to talk, think, and pray together.
- **c.** Once a year on a special date with a gift. Whether the gift is a book, a plaque, or a note that lets your son know how you have enjoyed and appreciated his friendship and growth, the gift becomes a special reminder of his relationship with you. This "gift date" may be a rite just before he finishes the school year, heading into the next grade.

2. *Plan and then participate in a one-on-one trip, just you and your son.* Together you look forward to and plan the outing for months. It could be a wilderness experience, a trip to a major league baseball weekend, or a tour of museums. What you do really doesn't matter. As each year goes by, invite your son to take on a bit more of the responsibility for the trip. During this stage, start with input on where to go, and each year increase involvement with planning, packing, and navigation.

3. *Increase your son's family duties to reflect his growing maturity.* Early adolescence is when you first move your son beyond the "normal" chores, those expected of him throughout his childhood years, such as cleaning his room or clearing the dishes, into a time of semi-employment, getting paid for more significant responsibilities.

Family responsibilities such as taking care of the lawn (mowing, trimming, "dog duty," or "dog dooty") or washing the cars every other week and being paid on a regular basis for such tasks, reflect what your boy will experience the rest of his life as an employee. This instills a sense of movement and responsibility that reflects a greater degree of trust than when he was a child.

4. *Let your son schedule how he spends his time.* Instead of a "Go do your homework" mentality and communication process, let your son know that once he hits middle school (or fifth or sixth grade; the actual year is not so critical) he is now responsible for his schedule, within the limits that you as a parent can live with. A good idea is to post this schedule so that times like play or down time, practice, television, homework, prayer and Bible study, and lights out are clearly displayed. This enables your son to stick to his schedule; he knows that as he hits this new phase of life, it is part of the territory (a rite!).

5. *Have your son join other family members in a "Serve the Family Day."* As we have already mentioned, serving is at the heart of our faith, and learning what it means to serve our family helps them to experience this truth where it is often the most difficult. During a monthly Serve the Family Day, each person in the family does something out of the ordinary to serve some other family member. Make a meal, rake some leaves, do an errand, stay home and baby-sit—it doesn't have to be much. It's simply a way of beginning to get the idea of serving those we love.

SCHOOL PLAYS

1. *Have breakfast and prayer at a local coffee shop once a month or so,* and then drop him off at school. This will give you a chance to help him to focus on how Christ desires to impact his daily life.

2. *Pray together on a regular basis for teachers and administrators.* Talk about who he likes, and who he doesn't, and why. Continue to encourage him to love those even though they may seem unlovable.

3. *Start the school year with a school march.* Here's an unusual ritual. Before each year begins, read Joshua 6 with your son. Then go together to the school where he will be attending and march around it, praying for the year. This may sound hokey, but it will have an impact on your son. When you finish the march, take your boy to a restaurant. There discuss what this event means, helping him to see that often God wants to do great things in and through us, and active prayer is one of the significant ways that He works.

4. *Ask your son at least every semester to plan a project* that can help him to serve Jesus at his school. It could be running for an office, organizing a schoolwide clean-up, or getting the basketball team to spend one day a month in the inner city serving the homeless. Or it could be some other project. Whatever he chooses, make certain that you connect this to God's compassion for people, especially the poor and broken, and how He usually uses us to touch them.

Social Plays

1. *Tell your son to start making decisions.* Though you must set the ground rules on time and activities, you should gradually allow your son to make his own choices. Taking greater responsibilities for activities during early adolescence is a helpful rite. Personal choice and experiencing the consequences when he doesn't follow through is valuable, even at this stage. If your son decides to participate in a sport, for example, he must set a schedule that reflects this choice, such as no time for TV (or a big reduction).

2. *With your son, establish clear guidelines for dating.* In many communities, kids at this stage begin to talk about (and even try out) dating. Many parents absolutely forbid this, using the argument that children are too young (at twelve years old or so) to "date." The reality, however, is that at this stage "dating" is rarely the same institution as parents knew it. It is our suggestion that your son be allowed to develop unique relationships with members of the opposite sex, as long as there are clear and established limits.

What are good guidelines for dating? During early adolescence we recommend that boys and girls spend no more than fifteen minutes a day on the phone with one person, that they only go on what can be called "group dates," where boys and girls travel to the activity in separate cars, and where there is adult supervision. Time spent in interaction at church youth groups, community choirs, and other public events are the healthiest forums for learning about the opposite sex at this age. But present your guidelines to your son for explanation and review. Let him know the reasons for them. This is a rite that prepares your son for the real dating days of middle and late adolescence.

3. *Help your son choose and evaluate friends.* Because learning how to develop deep and lasting friendships is vital during adolescence, a good idea is to encourage our sons to focus on a circle of good friends. About once a quarter, sit down with your son and ask him what he thinks are the qualities of a good friend. Encourage him to make a list, and you also make your own list. Each of you then writes down who you think fits this concept of a good friend. Pray for these people together and brainstorm how you can be proactive in deepening these relationships.

You may worry about this rite, especially if you feel that your son is in the "wrong crowd." But this suggestion can help him learn how to choose friends that are the healthiest for him as a person and a believer.

4. *Conduct Talk Times with your son.* Early adolescence marks one of the cruelest times in all of life. We can help our son to see this time of life as a challenge to be different. When you sense his need, call for a Talk Time: Ask your son to tell you who is being talked about, or laughed at, among his friends. Listen to him and pray with him, trying to come up with creative ways to protect that friend, or at least be a source of comfort in the midst of pain and loneliness.

If he is one who gets attacked and ridiculed, getting him to focus on those others who are victims will help him see that the best way to grow through this time standing tall is to help and care for others who need it. Instead of being a bystander or even a victim, your son can respond positively, with love and forgiveness.

INTERIOR PLAYS

1. *Encourage your son to begin a journal.* For most early adolescents, taking the time to sit down and write out thoughts and feelings is not something that comes easily. At this stage, just to get your son thinking about regular journaling is a healthy start. A dad can give his son a gift of a Bible and some sort of devotional book that directs a student's journaling when he hits this stage.

2. *Give your son the freedom to be alone.* Times alone—ideally in his own private bedroom—give him a sense of identity and wholeness. Even when your son exhibits intense emotions, outbursts, or mood swings, allow him the freedom to get alone and calm down. But then be sure to follow up. Once he is calm, ask direct questions that get to the root cause of the frustration. Most often it is not the obvious that is the issue; it comes from some other place of insecurity or anxiety.

3. *Teach your son to respect the humanity of the opposite sex.* At this stage, most often the issues surrounding your son's sexual development are far more identified with the interior area of his life than social. A helpful goal during adolescence is that your son recognizes that women are people to be cherished, esteemed, and treated with kindness, as opposed to being a means to sexual gratification. Do a Bible study with your son on sexuality, focusing primarily on 1 Thessalonians 4 and Matthew 5:27–28. Ask your son to rewrite these passages in his own words, and discuss their meaning as it relates to being a man who relates to women. Refer back to this work when your son begins to "go out with" a girl, reminding him of God's desire for him to stay pure in his relationship with girls/women.

Faith Plays

1. *Perform service projects together in Christ's name.* As you work side by side in ministry with your son, he has the chance to witness your faith at work. What you value and how your faith impacts your life will be right there on the surface when you are serving at a soup kitchen or cleaning an inner-city neighborhood. Let him also observe your own service projects, such as tutoring a fatherless elementary school child or helping an elderly neighbor clear leaves from the gutter.

2. *Memorize together a Scripture every week.* Memorizing biblical passages together enables your son to recognize the centrality of the Scriptures in our lives as mature followers of Christ. This, of course, is only one of many ways you can have a "quiet time" with your children. Whatever you do for devotions, the most important thing to remember is the actual activity is not as important as the sense of reality and authenticity with which it is displayed.

3. *Encourage and assist your son in being involved in a church youth group.* Without pushing your son, encourage him to connect with other believers. Volunteer (perhaps alternating with your wife) to drive him to activities. Help him raise funds so he can go to a youth retreat. You may even want to host preteens at your home. (Let the youth leader know your home is available.) By building solid friendships with Christian peers and committed youthworkers, your son will have a chance to deepen his own faith in the context of community apart from your family. This enables the individual identity to begin to form within the context of his faith.

The key to rites and rituals during early adolescence is emphasizing activities that develop a relationship of trust, friendship, and intimacy. Are you a father who wants to help your son across the bridge from boyhood to manhood? Then take advantage of these crucial years to show him that, as he grows up, you are committed to being there for him, as his friend as well as his dad.

EIGHT

MENTAL NOTES: AGES 13–15

J ust wait until they're teenagers!" This common warning echoes in the minds of many parents as they raise their children through the first twelve to thirteen years of life. The warning typically comes from those who have already been there, so their credibility is often unquestioned by the uninitiated.

There is fear as we anticipate the awful transformation that must take place when our children hit their thirteenth birthday. We half expect them to become a modern-day Mr. Hyde, popping out from behind the kitchen table with fiery darts in their eyes that say, "Now you're going to get it!" To hear some parents tell it, this is the time of life when alien life forms invade your child's bedroom at night and mysteriously take over his body and mind. According to traditional folklore, your mission is to try to survive the next few years without locking either yourself or your son in a closet.

In the next three chapters, we want to walk into the world of the midadolescent—those boys who are approximately thirteen to fifteen years old. Note that the early- and midadolescent years overlap. Depending upon puberty and other factors, a child may enter midadolescence at his thirteenth birthday or up to twelve months later. It's an interesting journey, and not without its dangers—but just how dangerous is it?

WHITEWATER RAPIDS OR FLOWING STREAM?

The reactions of several teenage boys during a junior high canoe trip along the American River in northern California reflect the excitement, turmoil, and growth of the middle adolescent years.

The Rapids

Most of the guys thought canoeing was a pretty macho thing to do, and several of the boys planned to show the girls what incredible studs they were. Rich, though, was on his first canoeing trip, apart from guided tours around the lake when he went to camp as an eight-year-old. Still, when he reached the river's edge, he was feeling pretty adventurous. As he put it, "I remember my excitement as we pushed our canoe out into the river and felt the current begin to carry us downstream with a quiet power."

Rich and fellow paddler Bob cruised along for about an hour, gaining ability in maneuvering their craft close to the girls' canoes without breaking the rules about running into each other. As far as Rich and Bob were concerned, everything was under control. Bob had canoed a couple of times before, and now Rich was feeling better at the paddle.

"Hey, Rich, this is cool. Looks like you've got the hang of things."

"Yeah, for sure. Hey, look at Jill and Ruth! Hey, where did you guys learn how to canoe? Sideways won't get you anywhere. Next thing you know, you'll be going backwards!"

Before they had entered the water, Rich, Bob, and the rest of the youth group listened to the leader's warning to be on the alert for certain spots along the river that churned wildly. These were not overly dangerous whitewater rapids, but they were challenging enough to test the best skills of beginning canoeists. I'll let Rich finish the story.

"We received instructions about how to make our way through these spots, and I paid close attention. 'If your canoe gets swamped and you end up in the water, swim with the current, not against it,' our leader told us. 'Otherwise, you'll just exhaust yourselves, because no one can fight the power of the river.' Later, we finally could see the whitewater ahead. Our canoeing arrogance dissolved quickly as we swallowed hard and braced ourselves for what was coming. All of a sudden we were there. The water churned and twisted as it raced over rocks that seemed to be everywhere. We worked hard to make it through and keep our canoe upright. Even Bob was happy for the instruction and suggestions that had been given.

"I guess I can be honest now. I questioned our ability, and Bob and I fought back our fears. We really tried to keep a cool facade for the others to see. It's a tough assignment to be panicking on the inside while playing it cool and confident on the outside. The funny thing was that everyone else was so busy trying to make it through the whitewater themselves that they didn't notice us."

Rich, Bob, and the others all made it through the whitewater with plenty of spray but little damage. Rich's canoe didn't dump them, but both had a few minor scrapes and bruises when they left the river. They laughed. Those actually became their badges of courage, and they showed them to anyone who'd ask. "Oh yeah," said Rich. "We looked death square in the eye, and lived to tell about it."

It is easy to make the mistake of assuming that all teenagers are like Rich's canoeing experience: They struggle through that whitewater. Many adults look at midadolescence as a stormy journey that must be endured, both by the growing teen and by parents. The teens may have occasional fun and games along the way, but inside there's frequent turmoil.

In the past, even the experts who studied and wrote about this time of life often made the same mistake. They frequently referred to this as a time of "storm and stress" in which teens experienced a tremendous amount of emotional upset and pressure. If they were able to ride out the storm, then they could move on to a more peaceful life.

Smoother Waters

The fact is, though, that many young teens do not experience emotional whitewater over which they feel they have no control. There is no question that all of them experience some amount of "whitewater" —but how much they experience, and how well they are prepared to handle it, is not the same for all. Different teens have different experiences—some panic, some don't. Some feel out of control, some don't. And there are plenty of teens who fall anywhere in between sheer panic and assured self-confidence.

There is a growing amount of evidence that a majority of young teens manage to make it through this period of life without significant, long-lasting trauma. While they experience varying degrees of struggle and challenge, most make it through with only minor emotional scrapes and bruises.

Do you know what makes the biggest difference in your son's ability to navigate the whitewaters of these midadolescent years? It's the same thing that helped us to make it through that river—preparation and instruction. Good preparation gives them some skills that can help them to avoid the rocks. And the first thing to know in order to help your son avoid the rocks of midadolescence is his mind. His thoughts are a lot different from when he was in early adolescence.

MENTAL NOTES: AGES 13–15

CHANGES IN THINKING

Jeff had always had a warm, close relationship with his fourteen-year-old son, Troy. Together, they had developed a number of common interests and hobbies over the years—bicycling and baseball card collecting were their favorites. When Troy was thirteen, his dad and he traveled to Michigan to ride in a fifty-mile bicycle tour. After a time of sweating and puffing, and lots of water, they finished; then they celebrated by attending a large card show in the same Michigan town.

But since that trip, Jeff began to notice some changes—changes that made him feel uneasy. Little by little, Troy began to withdraw from their shared interests. Troy's requests to do things with his dad virtually disappeared. Jeff missed those times, and he kept inviting Troy to work on their card collection or go on bike rides—invitations that were just as likely to get a no as a yes response. It now seemed as if Troy would rather spend time alone in his room listening to music or going out with friends than doing things with his dad.

It was Troy's attitude that bothered Jeff the most, though. His enthusiasm often gave way to indifference, and conversations became sprinkled with sarcasm. When Jeff asked Troy if there was anything wrong, his terse reply was usually, "No, nothing."

As Jeff came to understand that the changes he was seeing in Troy are a fairly common occurrence for midadolescent boys, he did a good job of working with Troy rather than against him. He did not excuse wrong behavior, but he also was wise enough not to try to cram obedience down his throat. What was it that Jeff learned about midadolescent boys? Let's take a look.

AN EXPANDING MENTAL WORLD

One of the biggest reasons that the relative tranquillity of the early adolescent years can give way to some unsettling changes is that your son's thinking is being transformed. He is gaining the ability to think in new ways—his mental world is expanding.

To a large extent, your son's thinking often still resembles that of a child. After all, that's the kind of thinking he knows best. He has been doing it for a number of years, and he has become good at it. Blending with this childlike thinking, however, are glimmers of more adultlike thinking. There are times when his insights may amaze you. His inexperience with this type of thinking, though, leads to a lot of mental miscues that will take time and experience to overcome.

More than anything else, he gains the ability to think about himself, others, and life situations in the abstract. He begins to recognize his own thinking. As one teen puts it, "I found myself thinking about my future, and then I began to think about why I was thinking about my future, and then I began to think about why I was thinking about why I was thinking about my future."[1] That kind of thinking gets confusing!

As he moves through this stage, the midteen gains an increasing sense of the way he thinks things should be, not just the way things are. He is now able to think not only in the present, but he can extend his thinking into the world of the "what if"—he can now reason in terms of what can be in addition to what is. This newfound ability affects how he communicates with others (including parents) and how he solves problems and makes decisions. The capacity to ask "What if . . ." will also affect how he looks at his faith and values. The result is new behaviors that are common to the midadolescent. As parents, we may think these behaviors are "bad," but in truth they are more irritating than bad and certainly should be understood as part of our sons' growing up. Several of these changes are described below.[2]

Off the Pedestal

A fundamental change in thinking is your son now takes authority figures off the pedestal. Perhaps Mark Twain summarized best this major change in thinking when he quipped, "When I was seven my father knew everything, when I was fourteen my father knew nothing, but when I was twenty-one I was amazed how much the old man had learned in those seven years." In case you missed it, the midadolescent is in the "my father knew nothing" stage! For most parents in healthy families, that statement is overkill, but there is a sense in which you are no longer the unquestioned expert. Your young son can give the impression that he now knows it all.

He can think about how people should be, not just how they are. He compares the real with the ideal, and takes note when they don't match up. He begins to realize that his parents, teachers, and other adults cannot measure up to what they say or who they should be—and he may find ways to let them know it. Many teens begin to see adults as equals—not in terms of power, but in terms of humanness. As equals, they begin to judge them according to a more critical standard.

Ready to Argue

Your young teenage son not only gains the ability to start thinking about possibilities, but his newfound ability to think about what should be can be reflected in questioning what he is told, especially by parents. What he accepted at face value when he was eleven or twelve years old is now open to challenge. He will debate; he will argue.

He begins to construct a picture of the way that life should be, often based upon what he wants. The questioning of your opinions and the challenging of your rules can create strained relationships at times. He views the world in terms of what should be by comparing who he is and what he can do with who his peers are and what they can do. For example, instruction to be home by a certain time when he was eleven or twelve years old will be accepted, even if it is not liked. At age fourteen, however, he may respond to being told to be back by 10:00 P.M. by asking why, questioning the fairness of the rule. The standard he often uses is the time that his friends must be home. The question of fairness is now a common argument, and it is usually used to his advantage.

What are the topics of disagreement with your son? If he is a mid-adolescent, chances are you are arguing about social issues—curfews, dress, music, hair styles, the telephone, and dating. Studies show that in healthy families, such social issues drive father-son debates.

In the "big picture" of life, most of these issues are pretty minor. More important are disagreements about major values, such as sexual behavior, religious attitudes, and attitudes toward drugs and alcohol; yet those are not usually a source of argument. In fact, most studies have found that, when teens and their parents are at odds over these major values, it usually is a result of problems in parent-child interactions that were present long before adolescence. [3]

While disagreements and conflict with a young teen are not welcome, a parent should regard all the questioning and challenging as an attempt to flex his new mental muscles. He is thinking at a new level, and he needs practice. And the safest and most accessible target for that practice is parents.

Unable to Decide

Your son may now have trouble making up his mind as he is confronted with decisions. His ability to think about possibilities makes him aware of just how many choices there can be. *What should I wear? What should I order off the menu? What should my friends and I do tonight?* Those thoughts and more tend to bind him as his life seems to be making one decision after another. Some are big, most are small, but always it seems he must decide.

MAN TO MAN

There are several ways we as dads can help our sons as they become increasingly self-conscious and try to establish their own
identities. Besides the cautions on pages 103–4, here are some suggestions for dealing with these changes:

His Self-Consciousness

1. *Don't play the game of twenty questions.* Respect his privacy by
   not always asking questions about personal activities. Your innocent question, "How was your day?" may not be so innocent
   to a fourteen-year-old. The more we grill our sons and try to
   pull information out of them the more they may clam up. To
   him, our questions may seem like prying.

2. *Do invite him to share with you on his terms and in his time.* When
   you "give him space," time to be by himself, he is more likely
   to come around and eventually let you in on what you want to
   know. Remember, your intense desire to know what is happening in his life collides with his need to be off stage and maintain
   his privacy. Let him come on stage when he is ready.

His Search for Identity

1. *Don't expect your son to cheerfully follow your direction for his life.*
   The old way of gaining his obedience won't work anymore. If
   we attempt to control his decisions and run his life, he will
   resist. Our son is growing up, and we need to change how we
   relate to him.

2. *Do recognize that your son does not enjoy conflict.* He does not
   want a verbal or emotional fight with us. The conflict that occurs reflects his pushing to become his own person.

3. *Look for creative ways for him to discover who he is and needs to
   become.* If we oppose his exploration, we will almost certainly
   guarantee conflict.

Mark has learned it's unwise to ask his sons where they want to eat when they go to a restaurant. It's especially bad when they go to "restaurant row," where the possibilities seem endless—fast-food spots, steak houses, all-you-can-eat buffets, Mexican, Chinese, and Italian. His boys have a difficult time making up their minds. He has learned that if he narrows the choice to only two or three restaurants, they have a much easier time making a decision.

If it seems farfetched to connect indecision to this newfound mental ability, consider children who have not yet acquired it. They just don't have the same problem. They typically have a favorite restaurant (usually fast food), a favorite food (maybe a hamburger, no matter how many choices the menu gives them), and they don't stand in front of a closet agonizing over what they should wear that day (or whether or not it all matches). Yes, it may be boring to you, but your little one finds order and delight in returning to the same place. The middle adolescent, however, wants choice, although he is not always sure what choice to make.

By the way, as you read the list above, maybe you identified with Mark's sons. Having a tough time deciding between a lot of choices is not necessarily something that gets easier with time. There are many older teens and adults who continue to have a difficult time making up their mind. That's because they, too, have that ability to imagine all the possibilities and mentally play with each one.

Inconsistent Behavior

There can be a large gap between the idealistic talk of a teenager and the behaviors they show. Thinking about the way things should be does not always translate into actions that match up with that thinking. Talk can be cheap.

One bystander remembers watching a group of teenagers in Rochester, New York, walk in a fund-raising event that would benefit environmental needs. The teens had raised dollar pledges for every mile they walked, and many walked proudly, seeing their walk as a way to support change and a better world. As David Elkind drove along the route, he felt a renewed hope as he watched the thousands of teenagers march for cleaner cities and a better environment.

The next day Elkind drove the same route and spotted city work crews cleaning up the large amount of litter that had been dropped by the walkers. The idealistic cause for which the young people marched and their own behavior told two different stories. We can only hope that the cost of the litter clean-up was not more than the amount of money raised for environmental clean-up![4]

Inconsistency also shows up in our own homes. Your teen may ask you to tell his brothers and sisters not to touch or use his things without getting permission. He wants them to respect his property and his privacy. When they don't, he gets mad, yells at them, and asks you to tell them again. On the other hand, your teen may feel free to use your shaver, stereo, tools, or any number of other things without getting your permission. Pointing out this inconsistency to him is not necessarily met with gratitude, either.

Conscious of Himself

Do you remember that fateful day as a young teenager when you woke up, looked in the mirror, and discovered that shiny red pimple in the middle of your forehead? You dreaded going to school, knowing that everyone there would notice your zit and talk about it behind your back. You either had to try to cover it up, put a Band-Aid® over it, and make up a story about how you got injured, or just gut it out while waiting for it to disappear.

There is a sense in which your son feels as if he is on stage, and that who he is and what he does is noticed and evaluated by others. Remember Rich and Bob? They were sure that everyone was watching what they were doing as their canoe hit that whitewater. This extreme self-consciousness is so strong in the junior high years that researchers have given it a name: imaginary audience. It is the belief that other people are as concerned about what you do, how you look, and thoughts that you have as you are.

Imaginary audience helps us to understand the increased desire and need for privacy that surfaces in young teens. It is only in the privacy of your son's bedroom or when he is by himself that he feels off stage. You need to respect your growing son's need for privacy. It is important to him.

THE SEARCH FOR IDENTITY

Most of the theories and much of the research that have been directed at adolescence have focused on the need for teens to establish an identity that is separate from their parents. It is important that your son be given the opportunity to begin to define himself as a separate person who has his own goals, dreams, and values. He needs opportunities to think about who he wants to be.

We need to see their new way of thinking and attempts at becoming their own person in the same way we saw their first attempts at walking. Rather than trying to hold our sons back and keep them from learning, we need to look for ways that encourage them to try—even though it's going to mean falling on their faces at times.

As dads, how we respond to those attempts to define themselves plays a key role in shaping the kind of relationship that we have with our sons at this age. Our sons are growing up, and we need to change how we relate to them. This is the trickiest part of parenting during this phase of adolescence.

Tom was a model son. He was gracious to adults, always polite, and was respectful every time his parents told him what to do. He never talked back, and his mom and dad believed everything he ever told them, because "Tom had never lied before," they loved to say. Both parents were fairly busy, he was the third child, and it was easier to believe that he could do no wrong. But Tom was the master of deception, the king of the "snow job."

In junior high, Tom and I (Chap) were best friends. He was fun and funny, and had a gleam in his eye that was attractive to all he met. I liked Tom, and admired the freedom he enjoyed due to his parents' trust in him, but I was always a bit nervous when I was with him. He didn't seem to have any sense of right and wrong, or any direction in how to make good decisions. With his friends, Tom was a wild man. He was the first guy I knew to get involved with sex, he constantly lied to his parents, and yet he knew that he had them wrapped around his little finger.

Because he was so "good," he was given incredible freedom for a teenager. He didn't have a curfew, there were no limits concerning money, or movies, or time on the phone, or relating to girls. Because of his ability to manipulate his too-busy parents, Tom had no limits. He became a machine of social experimentation. To Tom, this was the greatest possible life—no parents to hassle him, no restraints on his freedom, life was an open field of opportunity.

Today Tom is a divorced father who rarely sees his kids. The last time I saw him, he seemed shallow and aimless. What was once an excitable free spirit had become a disenchanted shell of a man. Though he seemed to enjoy the freedom his folks gave him, I always felt that Tom was out to prove himself, to be liked and admired by everyone he met. As I think about him now, I wonder if Tom was crying out for his parents to call his bluff.

If his dad had taken the time to see through his smoke screen and had cared for him enough to slow him down and give him limits within the context of an authentic, vibrant relationship, would Tom be different today? Would his marriage have lasted? Would he be more involved with his kids? Would he still have a passion for life? There is no way to know for sure, but I have a hunch. The freedom Tom had ultimately let him down. He never had the chance to discover his own identity and learn how to make wise choices, because he was given just enough rope to hang himself.

Proper Boundaries

How do you know which boundaries are appropriate for your son? For most of us, there are two extremes we need to avoid. First, we need to avoid the extreme that Tom's dad used. If you listen only to your son, the boundaries you set will be equal to the most lenient of any parent in town. Have you ever heard, "But Josh's parents let him stay out until midnight on weekends!" or "Everybody gets to go to R-rated movies, dad!" Such arguments may properly cause you to evaluate your position; but don't forget, dad, this is not Josh standing in front of you.

Each family, and each boy, is unique. What other parents do cannot be your ultimate criterion for setting boundaries. When your son shouts, "Justice!" and wants to compare, you can reply "just us," and remind him that each family is unique and accountable only to each other (not to others).

The second extreme, however, is to be so rigid with our rules that our son is given no room to negotiate. We've heard more than a few parents who have stated in one way or another, "No dating until he's eighteen, and that's final!" or "I don't care what other parents do, I'm not budging on this one." The older your son gets, the more he needs to be a part of the decision-making process. He needs some walls, the comfort that boundaries and limits bring. As the saying goes, "give him rope, but not enough to hang himself." But he also needs to be encouraged to develop his own sense of identity and control.

Balance, dad, that's the key. Talk to your son. Negotiate with him. Don't allow your schedule, or his ability to push your buttons to keep you from your task. He needs you to give him room—to explore, to experiment, to fail—but he also needs you to keep your eye out for him as he takes his first adult baby steps.

Working as a Team

The evidence is strong that teens are willing to cooperate with their parents and accept their guidance if they don't feel as if they are being dominated. That doesn't mean there won't be complaining or testing, but working as a team is possible.

Finding his identity—discovering who he is and what he wants to be—will be a much easier task if we work as a team. Your role, dad, is primarily one of support, encouragement, unconditional love, and challenging your son to think, evaluate his thinking, and live with the consequences of his decisions.

We need to find ways to help our boys think about the decisions that they are making. We need to give them practice in using their newfound mental abilities. When we can relate to our sons in a way that listens to what they are thinking, and are sensitive to how they feel, we will find that they are often willing to let us into their world and talk with us about their struggles.

Discuss the Issue

One of the best ways of gaining their cooperation and reducing disagreements is to shift from giving them commands to asking them questions wherever possible. Discussing the pros and cons of an issue with them will be more effective than trying to tell them what to do. That does not mean that they will always make wise decisions or come to value your wisdom. Remember, they are new at this and need practice. But gaining the ability to make wise decisions comes from making bad decisions and having to live with the consequences.

Suppose you want to teach your son to be a great tennis player. You can sit him down and talk with him at length about how to play the game. You can explain the rules of the game, how to hit the ball, and teach him strategy. But telling him about the game is never going to make him a great player. Until he picks up a racket and begins to practice hitting the ball, no amount of head knowledge is going to do him any good.

The same is true of responsibility and decision making. We can talk to our son about being responsible and making good decisions all we want. But until we start creating opportunities for him to practice responsibility and decision making, he'll never be any good at it. The sooner we start, the better. Give your son responsibility for running his own life in doses that he can handle.

Learning to work with rather than against our son's new abilities to think about things is not just important for minimizing conflict. It is important that we have a vision for our son of godly maturity marked by responsible decision making. Maturity and decision making is forged in experience, not in talking about it. Give him the experience!

NINE

DIFFERENT IS DANGEROUS

One summer I (Chap) spoke at a junior high Christian conference in Bristol, Tennessee, called "The Great Escape." Imagine for a minute what an escape it is for a middle-aged seminary professor to spend a week speaking to and hanging out with eight hundred middle adolescents. Having been with teens for several years of youth ministry, I didn't feel fear, but I also was unsure what I would encounter.

Soon after arriving with my family, I realized that I had little to worry about. As I walked and watched, talked and played, I was reminded that at this stage kids are far more worried about how they look and who they know than they are about what they think of somebody else's dad who talks to them at night.

During this week my fear was replaced with joy at having the chance to be around them, share a bit of my life with them, and let them know that God loves them right now, as they are, not as they think they need to be. What a privilege for this middle-aged professor!

The social scene of the middle adolescent is full of risks. In fact, middle adolescence is considered the most dangerous of the three adolescent stages. Experts know it, research confirms it, and parents and youth workers see it. Here teens encounter many social and psychological risks—risks that carry potentially negative consequences if things do not go well. It is a time of choices, and sometimes there is not a lot of thought given to the consequences of those choices. Those choices actually are more important than the circumstances.

As we mentioned in the last chapter, we need to help our sons make good choices during this stage. But for the majority of boys,

DIFFERENT IS DANGEROUS

puberty has now hit full force, and changes in thinking create a number of challenges that must be met. Boys are maturing into men and feel different—and different is dangerous, with confusion and fear appearing from time to time.

But the picture is not all gloomy. Many teens journey through this stage with a minimum of developmental bumps and bruises. We will look shortly at those factors found to contribute to an easier transition for midteens; first, we need to understand what is happening in the lives of these teens.

As with the early adolescent (chapter 6), social changes are underway, as these eight characteristics show.

A QUICK SKETCH

Middle adolescents share several personal attitudes and social characteristics during this stage.[1] Keep in mind that these eight characteristics are closely connected to the changes in thinking discussed in chapter 8.

1. *A Strong Need for Independence.* Middle adolescents are a long way from being able to handle life completely on their own, but often it's hard to convince them of that fact. They feel capable of making their own decisions. As a result, they hate to have to ask for permission to do anything. They would prefer to announce what they are doing.

2. *Reduced Communication with Parents.* The need to separate from parents and protect their personal life outside the family results in less parent-child communication. Parents may feel as if they have to pull information out of their son—but the more they pull, the less they may get. Teens want to communicate on their own terms.

   The communication that does happen centers on them. They are not likely to ask you as a parent about events in your life—they are too consumed with what's happening in their own lives. They are also likely to interpret your comments in ways that suit their purposes. A charge of "You just don't understand" more often means "You don't agree with me," or "You're not telling me what I want to hear," than it means you don't understand.

3. *A Know-It-All Attitude.* Out of the wisdom that parents have gained through experience, it is understandable that they want to guide their sons with helpful advice that will spare them from making mistakes or getting hurt. Teenagers are anxious to soak up this advice, right? Wrong! Unsolicited advice from parents is as welcome as ants at a picnic. They are apt to shrug it off with an "I already know

DIFFERENT IS DANGEROUS

that." Their know-it-all attitude can also show up in smart-aleck remarks or verbal put-downs of others.

4. *More Time Spent Alone*. Teens love to spend time with friends, but they also love to spend time by themselves. There is a need for privacy and being "off stage." Retreating to a bedroom for hours at a time meets these needs.

5. *Sudden Mood Changes*. One of the toughest things for parents to handle during this stage is the rapid and unpredictable changes in emotion that can take place. Their son may be pleasant and on top of the world one moment, and irritating and depressed the next. Angry flare-ups or "silent treatment" can seem to come from out of nowhere, and may disappear as quickly as they come.

6. *A Here-and-Now Pleasure Orientation*. Attempts to get teens to think about the future or delay gratification of their desires can be futile. Teens live for the moment, and the watchword for life is fun. Things that are not fun, like homework or household chores, are to be endured (and if possible, avoided). That means planning is not as important as doing, and sometimes midteens do not want to wait to have or do things.

7. *Acceptance Based on Externals*. Teens want to have the right clothes, the right hairstyle, and the right behaviors. Membership in a peer group calls for a strong conformity to its external markers. Teens may nag parents to bankroll their shopping needs in order to maintain their status.

8. *An Upturn in Personal Grooming*. Remember the days when you had to fight to get your son to take a bath? You probably won't need to fight him on that one anymore. This may be related to the puppy love incentive, which says that "the dirt indelibly bonded to your son's elbows since he was five will mysteriously disappear just before his first date."[2] It also may relate to his desire not to be a misfit, a social outcast of the group.

   A total lack of concern for appearance now turns to an intense awareness of how one looks. Bathroom time increases. Personal appearance has to be just right before going out in public. Depending on the style, he may even shape his hair to look as if he just got out of bed, but rest assured he has spent time making it look that way.

The above eight characteristics may not look like a formula for warm, fuzzy family times. Actually, those times are possible. But we have to be willing to create the right conditions for them to occur, and then allow our teen to decide when to cooperate with those conditions.

RELATIONSHIPS WITH FAMILY

Most parents who are enjoying their younger children have heard the curse muttered by at least a few seasoned veterans: "Just wait until your kids are teenagers!" Those former parents of adolescents seem to imply there is this viral infection called *parentus tormentus* that strikes every growing child on his or her thirteenth birthday. Symptoms of being infected supposedly include such things as dislike for parents, rebellion, and generally making the parents' world a living nightmare. The reality is that the forecast does not often match the facts.

While it may surprise you, all of the available evidence shows that most midadolescents feel close to and positive about their parents. They can have a funny way of showing it sometimes, though. Studies indicate that only about 20 percent of families have serious conflict with their teen, and those families were usually having a lot of problems before the child ever approached adolescence.[3]

Independent, Yet Dependent

Teens in healthy families tend to hold similar values to their parents, and they have a strong need for their parents to approve of them. Your son wants support and direction from you, but he may act in ways that send an opposite message. While his desire is for independence, he is still dependent at heart. Underneath that tough, confident exterior are a bundle of fears and insecurities. Don't let his behavior fool you—his armor-plated self-esteem is more like cardboard than steel. Many parents have learned the hard way how easy it is to hurt their son and shatter his facade.

Teens are not the only ones whose desires and actions do not always match up. As we try to communicate with our sons, we often make the same mistake that our sons do. We send double messages because of our ambivalence about wanting our sons to grow in independence, but also wanting them to remain dependent. We say one thing, but we do another.

I remember the time that Trevor wanted to get one of those sports tape players that you clip on your belt—the ones with the stereo headphones that let a teen turn up the volume and shut out the world, including parents. He looked in catalogs, he checked them out whenever we went to a store, and he kept saving his money. He had his eye on a model that, to me, seemed like a smart choice.

DIFFERENT IS DANGEROUS

But then teenage reality set in. There was a big sale on a cheaper model—and I do mean cheaper. Trevor decided that he had waited long enough, and so he announced that he was going to buy the sale model. He had been saving for a while, and I hated to see him "waste" his money on a product that screamed, "Don't buy me—I won't last!" So I decided to give him the benefit of my wisdom. My intentions were good—I was looking out for his best interests.

If you haven't already guessed it, my wisdom was not received with open arms. In fact, our discussion became what I would call animated, with voices starting to rise. Finally, Trevor looked me in the eye and said, "Dad, you're always saying how you want me to be independent and make my own decisions, but right now I feel like a little kid who's being told what to do. Which way do you want it?" He was right. My words said one thing, but my actions were saying another. For years I have been encouraging him to make more and more of his own decisions, and I have come to trust what he usually does with that responsibility. I backed off, and he bought the sale recorder.

His decision may have been a bad one, but which one of us doesn't have to learn from our own bad decisions at times? We learn to make good decisions by making bad ones. Experience is a great teacher. While we need to protect our kids from emotionally damaging decisions, we also need to let them learn from their mistakes. (By the way, the recorder he bought turned out to be a good one. It lasted a long time and gave him countless hours of enjoyment. Sometimes Dad's wisdom is not all-wise).

Showing Support and Warmth

Balancing your son's desire for independence and the need for parental guidance can be tough. "Walking the Balance Beam," the Man to Man application for this chapter, gives some suggestions. One suggestion for keeping the balance is to display warmth and support for your son. Unfortunately, surveys of teens have found that fathers are often perceived as emotionally distant and impersonal.

At times showing warmth may be very tough on you, dad. Some days he will be your friend, your buddy with whom you can laugh and banter, pray and hug. Other mornings, though, he may seem to be an impersonal tenant whom you have severely offended. The worst part in this is it can change from day to day, sometimes hour to hour. It is during these times that you as his father may have the hardest time being a pillar of warmth and caring for your son. But it is important for you to recognize that this type of behavior is often part of the package of middle adolescence, and your son needs to know you are for him even when he gives you the cold shoulder.

The experience of successful fathers has demonstrated the effectiveness of negotiation with teenagers. An attempt to dictate and control a teen's behavior is a sure recipe for conflict. Teens are often more open to your guidance when they feel that they have input into decisions. They are also more likely to abide by standards that they have helped to decide. This negotiation process can also create mutual understanding, a sense of cooperation, and a stronger relationship.

Real life is often messier than theory, however. Negotiation does not always work—and that can be the fault of dad, son, or both. Finding solutions that make both father and son happy is often hard work. But it's worth it. The evidence is clear—a warm, loving dad who can listen to and understand his son's opinions while reserving the right to make final decisions does the best job of promoting healthy development in his son. And that's no small accomplishment.

RELATIONSHIPS WITH PEERS

Do you want to strike fear into the heart of a parent? If he has a midadolescent, turn to him and whisper in his ear just two words: *peer pressure.* While we are concerned with what other people think of us at every stage of life, a parent soon learns that what people think is never more important than it is to a middle adolescent.

Inside the head of every midadolescent, one question repeats itself: Do you like me? Teens at this stage want everyone to like them, and they expend energy to try and make that happen. They associate with other kids hoping to answer this question positively. That sense of acceptance—or rejection—by his peers is the most powerful shaper of a child's identity at this stage. The possibility of being rejected by peers is a real fear. Teens who do not identify with a peer group have been found to have a strong sense of isolation, loneliness, and worthlessness.

If we are concerned with our child's Christian faith, we will make sure that our midadolescents have solid groups to which they can belong, such as church youth groups and ministries like Youth for Christ or Campus Crusade.

This strong need to belong and be accepted results in two predictable consequences: group conformity and what we call "parental leprosy." (The second sounds painful, but don't worry, it does pass away.)

WALKING THE BALANCE BEAM

H onoring your son's desire for independence while recognizing his need for parental guidance is like walking a balance beam. The problem is that you can fall off either side. Most dads err in one direction or the other. Some allow their sons so much freedom and independence that the boys are left to wonder why there are no limits. John, a junior high boy, would brag in public about having no rules from dad and mom to follow. In the privacy of a counseling session, however, this tough guy sat and cried, saying, "You know, just once I wish my parents would have enough guts to say no." Other dads are just the opposite, directing every aspect of their children's lives. They relate to their son as if he were still a small child, giving him advice, commands, and directives. It's tough to "stay on the beam" and avoid these two mistakes.

It may not be possible to maintain this balancing act in a way that is satisfying to both you and your son, at least not all the time. But we should try to stay on the beam as much as we can, knowing that we can always climb back on after a fall.

Two effective strategies for staying on the beam are:

1. Offer your son a strong dose of warmth and support.
2. Negotiate boundaries and areas of decision making.

Hopefully, the warmth and support have been built into your relationship from the time he was a little boy. That needs to continue, even when you don't feel like it.

Group Conformity

Remember your junior high school days? For those of us who survived the sixties, it consisted of madras shirts that "bled" when they were washed, bell bottom pants, long hair, and classic music with titles like "Feelin' Groovy" and "I Am the Walrus." We also had a language system that adults could not decipher. If they did manage to decipher it, it was an unwritten rule of the Junior High Juvenile Code of Ethics that the system then be changed immediately. Fitting in was all-important.

Hair styles, clothing, and music have all changed since then, but some things don't. The junior high crowd still has its own language (and now we can't decipher it), and it still has its own standards that every kid must conform to. These markers that signify belonging help to give your son a sense of identity—identity that is different from his parents.

The powerful influence of peers is a source of anxiety for parents. Today the pressures for teens can be strong—sexual experimentation, smoking, drinking, drugs, and even vandalism or violence. And the primary factors that contribute to these problems are the need to belong and the pressure to conform.

There is reassuring news. Studies have consistently found that teenagers do not reject their parents' values. That's right. As we have noted before, if you have a loving relationship with your son, and you look at what you argue about with him, you will most likely find tension about social issues—hair or clothing, curfews, music, or social activities. And, for the most part, it will be peers that your son uses to make decisions about these areas.

When it comes to values, however, teens from loving families look to their parents. Their ideas about morality, education, careers, and faith are more like than unlike that of their parents. And teens most often look to their parents for advice and modeling when it comes to questions or confusion about these values. While there are undoubtedly some exceptions, these trends are so strong that most experts agree that there is something seriously wrong in family relationships where a teen rejects everything that his parents stand for.

So, dad, you are not powerless during this stage. Peers do exert a strong influence on your son, but so do you. In fact, the best predictor of who your son chooses for friends, and which teens he listens to, is you. The relationship that you have with him affects which teens will influence him. Your son will tend to find friends that are already like him, they will all influence each other to become even more like each other, and their alikeness will give them a sense of security and belonging.

Parental Leprosy

Little boys love to sit on their dad's lap. As they get bigger, they often still like to be hugged and feel close. But if you are the father of a middle adolescent, you have probably discovered that there is a disease known as parental leprosy.

You most likely discovered this disease at some point when you were in public with your son. While trying not to be too disrespectful, your son doesn't seem exactly proud to be seen with you when his friends are around. He may even give you instructions beforehand about not "embarrassing" him—which can be defined as anything that shows he belongs to you.

If you go to an athletic contest or a movie, he sits in a seat that is mathematically the farthest away from where you are sitting. You don't really need to wear a disguise, you just need to pretend that you don't know him. Joke with him, saying "Hey, you don't mind if I sit by you when I get there, do you?" or "I got a big good-bye hug waiting in these arms" and watch the reaction. You'll chuckle, and he'll stare at you like you're Benedict Arnold's cousin.

Phil tells of the time he and his wife took their son to a football game. When they arrived at the game, Phil's son announced, "I'm going to stay in here and finish my hamburger." As the parents got out of the car, Angie turned to Phil and asked, "Is there anything wrong?" He replied, "No, if he walks with us, it will create an awkward situation for him, and then he'll need to find some excuse to leave." Sure enough, about five minutes later, he walked down in front of them, and went clear to the other end of the stands and sat with some other kids.

Again, as mom watched this scene unfold, she wanted to know if anything was wrong. Dad replied, "Absolutely not. He's normal."

What a wise dad! Phil recognized that parental leprosy is not a sign of real sickness. In fact, if you think back to when you were a mid-adolescent, you were probably the same way.

If your relationship is healthy, you will notice that the leprosy goes into remission when you are at home or somewhere safely away from the gaze of other teens (or at a public event when he needs money!). Your cooperation with this need in your son's life will be greatly appreciated, and it may even yield some close interactions at home. That may give you the opportunity to talk about another emerging reality for your young teenage son—girls.

DIFFERENT IS DANGEROUS

Relationships with the Opposite Sex

The indifference of early adolescence gives way in the middle years to hormone-driven interest when it comes to girls. Midadolescent boys gain a sharply focused awareness that girls are designed with a differently shaped body than boys, and they like the difference. This interest is reflected in the finding that the average age at which later teens and adults report they had their "first love" is fourteen.

This Thing Called Romance

As with all other developmental milestones we have discussed, midadolescents are new at this thing called romance. They are what we call "love toddlers." They test their abilities by talking with friends, comparing themselves to others, and making trial-and-error forays into the world of dating. As they fall on their relational noses at times, they gradually become more skilled with opposite-sex interactions. Because they are love toddlers, their efforts can be cute, and sometimes amusing, to those of us who have long since learned to "walk" and put those days behind us.

The thinking and relationships of this stage are well-represented in the questions that junior high teens ask about dating. Dads are likely to hear one of the following during the middle years of adolescence:

"How can you get others to like you?"

"What do boys look for in a girl?"

"Do you have to follow everybody else to be popular?"

"What do you do if you're scared to ask a girl to go on a date?"

"Why shouldn't a girl call a boy if she wants to?"[4]

They are interested in establishing relationships, but they are naive about how to go about doing that. As you will see in late adolescence, the questions change as they get older.

The TV series "The Wonder Years," which followed its main character, Kevin Arnold, from age eleven to seventeen, had good insights into middle adolescence. Often viewers could listen in to the thoughts of Kevin. In one episode, after an especially confusing exchange at junior high school with his girlfriend Winnie, he concluded, "That's when I discovered that love was going to be a lot more complicated than I had imagined."

Most midadolescents are still trying to learn that truth, for they tend to romanticize boy-girl relationships, seeing relationships as easier and less complicated than they are. Young love is a combination of romanticized imagination and identification with one's friends. Tune in

DIFFERENT IS DANGEROUS

to a teen radio station at night and listen to the young teens call in with their dedications to girlfriends and would-be girlfriends. Love songs abound. It is an education in middle adolescent relationships.

We heard an Indiana radio station that features a nightly song dedication segment. On "Slow Jam," teens would call in and pledge their "undying love." But these were not individual dedications—they were group dedications. One night Mark called in with this dedication, "Yea, I want to dedicate this song to Kathy, and also make it from Chad to Samantha, Jim to Michelle, and Leslie to Paul. And Heather, will you go out with Matt if he asks you?" Such is young love—couples within groups, trying to impress, be included, and to win approval.

Feelings of "love" can be strong, even if the boy hasn't gathered the courage to talk to the object of his affection. One young girl answered yes when asked if she had a boyfriend. "His name is Jason, and I love him very much. . . . Yeah, I have a notebook filled with hearts and doodles and our names inside."

Interestingly, she explained that Jason and she had never been on a date, never talked about liking each other, and never spent time together alone. They did talk with each other in the hall at school and hung out with some of the same friends. Such is young love—love without real relationship.

Not Every Boy Will

Of course not all midadolescents date; in fact a significant proportion have little desire to go through traditional "dating." This does not mean that they are "weird" and certainly not that they have homosexual interests. Boys choose not to date at all or very little during their junior and even high school years, and their reasons for not developing romantic relationships are often very healthy. For instance, they may feel that pursuing a girl can hurt school studies; they may have lots of extracurricular activities, such as sports or school clubs; they may think it requires a lot of money they don't have; or they may work part time.

And, of course, there may be fear of rejection. Boys at this stage are still forming their own sense of identity, and dating can be frightening for some boys. Love your son as he is, and for most boys this will take care of itself.

As teens move toward the end of this stage, however, many do date, and others begin to move more toward pairing off in couples and even going steady. Traditional dating becomes more common, prompting parents to set new boundaries.

Midadolescent Coaching

These excursions into the world of "love" are a normal experience for young teenage boys and girls. How you react to these experiences will affect not only your relationship with your son, but also his sense of who he is as a male. Put-downs, sarcasm, or telling him he is too young to understand real love will not work.

Bruce Baldwin, a practicing psychologist and author on parenting, has suggested that parents need three important qualities in dealing with their sons and helping them through this second stage of adolescence.[5] These qualities are:

1. *"Depth" perception.* A father needs to be able to see below the surface when he watches his son. Look below the outer mask. Don't make the mistake of assuming that your son's show of confidence or independence or resistance is all there is. Look for the real feelings and insecurities that are there.

2. *Consistency of response.* Your son lives with inconsistency as a young teenager. While he may not even realize it, he needs a source of stability and strength in a world that can seem overwhelming and pressured. You can be that source.

3. *Inner conviction.* There are few times in your parenting life that you will need to be more sure of your own values. As a father, you need to know what you believe, why you believe it, and what is important to you. Your son may challenge who you are and what you stand for—either in actions or in words. You need to be able to answer that challenge.

Middle adolescence is a time of awakening, a time of coming into manhood, a time of testing the waters of autonomy and identity. It's like that weird joke, so typical of junior high humor: "Did you hear about the skeleton who went into the soda shop and demanded, 'I'd like a root beer, and a mop!'?" Like that skeleton, your son wants to drink up life, and yet he is bound to spill it all over himself at times. Celebrate with him as he takes these giant leaps into manhood. It can be fun for both of you!

TEN

THE MIDADOLESCENT PLAYBOOK

R emember the "Early Adolescent Playbook" in chapter 7? Things may seem simpler in that playbook compared with this one. The main reason is that your son's life was simpler then. He still identified himself as a member of the family—his identity remained rooted in his relationship to the family and as your son. Many of his interactions occurred there. Now, at the middle-adolescent stage, he begins the process of establishing a sense of self and a genuine identity apart from the family as well. Adolescence, remember, is marked by the need to be needed as well as the need not to be needed.

The Early Adolescent Playbook need not be tossed out the bedroom window, though. Those rites still remain important markers in his march toward manhood. However, new plays are needed to supplement your approach. We have to face it as men: during middle adolescence the father-son relationship faces its greatest strain. You as the father may have a difficult time understanding why your son used to love to do things together, have (relatively) substantive conversations, and basically "hang out," and now does few of these things.

AVOIDING THE WEDGE OF SEPARATION

Although adolescence has always tended to pull parents and sons apart, in our culture there are two factors that drive the wedge even deeper. The first is a father's lack of understanding about what his son is experiencing during these years. A major purpose of *Boys to Men* is to give fathers the tools to better understand their sons. When we fathers don't realize that what our sons are going through represents a normal developmental process, we often become less tolerant and easily frustrated and discouraged during this middle stage of adolescence. For most dads, the response is withdrawal, which in turn causes an internalized guilt and ultimately a painful sense of loss.

The second issue that causes conflict in the father-son relationship during this period is a father's lack of time and energy required to break through the perceived rejection of him by his son. If a dad doesn't realize how important his relationship is to his son, especially during this time of relational transition and confusion, a deep rift could occur in the relationship, which sometimes can be irreparable.

The father who is aware of both of these issues, however, is on the way to helping his son traverse the difficult path of middle adolescence. Though at times it may be a stormy and rocky road, the father who walks with his son, sometimes in front showing the way, and sometimes behind allowing him to take the lead, has the best chance of growing his son into mature and godly manhood.

During this period of middle adolescence, a boy is beginning to feel the effects of pulling away from his family. It is culturally natural, and it has been proven over the centuries and cultures that God designed this transition to take place. But it is not easy, especially for the boy. He longs to be free from parental control and authority, to establish his own identity and autonomy, yet he still longs to sit on your lap and listen to your stories. The little boy has not quite let go, while the young man pushes to break away.

Continuing to Build

The Middle Adolescent Playbook contains suggestions for rites and rituals in bringing a boy through middle adolescence to appropriate maturity. Again, these ideas do not stand alone; they assume that you are continuing to build on the suggestions presented in chapter 7, The Early Adolescent Playbook. Parents who incorporate a lifestyle of rites and rituals as the means of growth for their son need not abandon those that have brought them through the early years of adolescent transition. These become ingrained in the everyday life of the family, and especially in the father-son relationship. The suggestions in this chapter, then, represent additional rites and rituals for the next level of development, growth, and maturity. As you implement them into the life of your family, add them as a supplement to the rituals already developed.

For the father who is discovering this parental strategy of rites of passage and family rituals while living with a middle (or even late) adolescent, we suggest that you first get your family used to the idea of family rituals by implementing a few ideas from chapter 7. Though some may seem too elementary and trivial to your middle adolescent, this strategy will provide a sense of continuity between rituals. We do encourage you, however, to move quickly to bring your son (and entire family) up to speed to the age-appropriate rites. Your son is ready for more than just a taste of manhood. He is now ready to take on some significant responsibility and authority.

The ideas found in this chapter are designed to complement and take further the ideas in chapter 7, to take your son a step closer to becoming a man in ways that fit his stage of development. Again, we do not recommend that you do everything, or even most of the ideas mentioned here, just try what fits. The Playbook begins on the next page.

Family Plays

1. *Grant a specific responsibility for a family event.* With the family rituals described in chapter 7, your son can now handle specific duties in family outings, trips, and events. This can be anything from navigating a vacation to handling the meal budget. Encourage your son to participate in every facet of the logistics and grant him a significant degree of responsibility, so that he will soon be prepared to handle the details of a trip on his own.

2. *Have him negotiate his work role in the family.* In both his weekly chores and other family duties, your son should be able to choose his responsibility. Instead of forcing him to be the designated lawn mower, for example, allow him to pick and choose from a variety of options, and let him know you expect him to therefore be committed to carrying out the entire task, on his own.

3. *Create a budget with him.* An allowance should have begun in early adolescence; now we go beyond the basics so he may learn more about budgeting, saving, spending, and tithing. Most experts believe that an allowance should not be tied to specific chores or even be used as disciplinary ammunition, but rather should be used as a tool to help your son to learn how to handle money. At this point, a monthly allowance, or one every two weeks (similar to a paycheck timetable), should be connected to a monthly "budget meeting" (e.g., responsibility for clothes, school lunches, etc.), where he must account for how he plans on managing the money he is given.

Remember, though, for this to be a marker, it is important that any parental input is merely advice, as opposed to a heavy-handed and authoritarian control. Helping your son think through his choices is helpful, but allowing him to get stuck, or overextended, is a far greater teacher. As a rule of thumb one last hint: Never grant an advance! (Does a corporate boss?)

School Plays

1. *Be a school dad.* Fathers can show they care about this key element of their child's life by joining the process. Your son is probably making choices about which classes to take and how to divide his time among studies, school activities, and recreation. Invite yourself to become a part of the process, again, as an advisor and confidant as opposed to a dictator. School dads don't direct; they listen and offer input. Pray through the semester's schedule, and discuss with him what will best prepare him for the future.

2. *Help your son to develop the journal habit.* Your son may have already begun the journal rite as part of his Early Adolescent Playbook for his interior plays. Now he can make the journal a rite of his school plays. Encourage him to keep a journal of what happens at school, both the highlights and lowlights, and discuss this weekly with him, asking him to read any portions he is comfortable revealing to you or issues he wants to discuss.

3. *Become a school prayer partner with your son.* During your one-on-one times together, talk about what difference it makes to be a Christian at school. Pray together for his struggles, and keep a journal of your prayers so that you can show him how God worked during the year at school.

4. *Have him plan a once-a-year (or semester) school project that can honor Christ.* During early adolescence, one ritual was performing some service project. That can continue during middle adolescence, though the type of project usually changes to reflect his growing maturity. Every project should honor Christ. One that does is tutoring younger students, or volunteering as a peer counselor. Help him to see that Jesus Christ is honored when a Christian serves others; though the activity may not be overtly "spiritual," he is living out Matthew 25.

Another project is for him to join a Christian campus club like Young Life or Fellowship of Christian Athletes. Here he can learn fresh ways to live out his faith, helping classmates and even learning how to bring others to Christ. He may also find new Christian friends here, which is part of his social growth.

Social Plays

1. *Make a date agreement.* This is the time when father and son should negotiate some clear guidelines for dating. Most middle-adolescent boys will have an increasing desire for a dating relationship (what we used to called "a steady"), so your son needs to be thinking about how to treat a girl as a friend, in a casual dating relationship, and as a "steady." This is the period where boys are notorious for their insensitivity toward girls. Set a clear standard for your son to seek to be different—to see girls as sisters, or potential sisters, in Christ.

As the two of you discuss a date agreement, be sure to bring up the biggies. Issues like kissing, petting, and allowing lust to have a foothold should be discussed openly. You may even find a need to mention certain explicit behavior if your son seems to have acquired much sexual knowledge through reading or talking with other boys. Help him to make specific decisions about boundaries to avoid impurity. Then help put it in either an oral or written agreement between you and him, man to man. As we have already mentioned, there are many good resources for helping your son in this area. However, it is primarily your job, dad, to help your son become a man of integrity in his dating life.

2. *Give your son a love token.* Present your son with some tangible symbol that will remind him of God's call on his life to be sexually pure. A love token tells him that he has committed to a moral standard that shows love for God, his father, the girl, and for himself.

One dad gave his son a class ring when he became a freshman in high school, inscribed with the biblical reference 1 Timothy 4:12. He talked with his son about what the ring and that verse stood for, and challenged his son to remember its significance as he became involved in dating relationships. He went on to recommend that his son wear the ring until he got married, and then present it to his wife with an explanation of how it represents the history of his sexual purity for her. That's a powerful love token.

3. *Create an entertainment zapper.* Teens are fairly sophisticated today when it comes to entertainment. They can take a TV remote and "surf" from channel to channel. Friends can invite them to watch a rented video or play a video game. Typically your son won't naturally consider the impact of what he watches, and curiosity may lead him to unhealthy fare. Discuss and negotiate movies, television, and even choice of music.

Because in this culture movies and cable TV are filled with images that threaten a boy's ability to control lust and sexual fantasizing, he needs to create an entertainment zapper. Recognize that you no longer can simply control and steer his choices. Don't "just say no," help him to make wise media decisions, so he will avoid those programs, movies, and video games that are unhealthy.

4. *Be part of the teen crowd.* No, we don't mean regress to your teenage years. Instead, invest in the lives of teenagers even as you invest in your son's life. Beyond knowing some of his friends, encourage a few of his close friends, primarily associated with your son's faith (church friends, or school friends who are Christians from other churches). Offer to facilitate a monthly outing with this group of guys to deepen their sense of community with one another.

INTERIOR PLAYS

1. *Develop together a plan for mutual disclosure.* During this stage many fathers retreat from intimacy with their sons, but your son needs exactly the opposite. This is the time to begin to develop a friendship of mutuality. Beware going too deep too quickly, but share with your son some of your struggles as a man, an employee, and as a Christian. There is a very fine line here, and the father who discloses too much risks undercutting his son's need for parental stability. The idea is to begin to develop a man-to-man style of vulnerability and communication, thus allowing your son to see you as a whole person, warts and all.

2. *Write your son a letter quarterly or when out of town.* Invite him to write you back. Your letter would include your feelings and impressions about life. A letter will enable you to communicate to your son feelings in a way that usually is more reflective than in everyday conversation. He can read and reread what you have to say to him, and he can keep the letter for years to come.

3. *Make an agreement to ask questions of your son.* When together, ask leading questions concerning the feelings your son is currently experiencing. In our culture, this era begins the cultural male tendency to "stuff" and ignore feelings, and helping your son acknowledge frustration, loneliness, and fear is a tremendous gift to him. Instead of, "How was your day?" ask, "What was fun for you today?" followed by "What was hard for you today?"

Faith Plays

1. *Find your son a mentor.* Pray for and pursue another man to come into your son's life. It may be a youthworker (paid or volunteer), an older gentleman in the congregation of your church, or a Christian neighbor, but another man's perspective on life and faith can help to solidify in your son that the faith of his family is real for others, too.

2. *Watch the news together.* Periodically watch the news or news documentaries. When the program is over, turn off the TV and discuss how a Christian is called to respond to the needs of a dark and broken world.

3. *Teach a Sunday school class together.* The relationship with your son will move toward a "coworker" position from simple father and son relationship when you work together on curriculum, and learn such things together as how to handle discipline in the class. This requires that you are committed inwardly to being your son's partner and friend, instead of ordering him around.

4. Go to a *Christian concert or other major event together.* You create a valuable source of common ground centered around Christ when you attend a Christian event he enjoys. The event could be a concert, a large-scale outreach program, or a youth training event. Such events are having a major impact on the lives of thousands of young people, and any parent who desires to help his son grow in Christ can use these as catalysts to further discussion and growth.

5. *Attend a Christian seminar or conference together.* Take your son to hear a well-known Christian speaker, or attend a Christian conference together; for example, Promise Keepers.

ELEVEN

MENTAL NOTES: AGES 16–18

I n most states, driver's training is given or learn-er's permits are issued for a period of time before a driving license can be obtained. A learner's permit gives a teenager the opportunity to learn to drive a car under the watchful eye of a parent or responsible adult who can sit alongside him and provide the teen with correction and instruction. Sane parents would never consider handing over the family car keys to a teenager who has never had some training behind the wheel.

The dad who wants to understand and help his son to grow men-tally can think of late adolescence as a time for a "thinker's permit." This is the final stage before adulthood, dad, and you can provide your son with intentional opportunities to get behind the wheel of his mind and practice adultlike thinking and decision making. Teens who grow into godly decision makers have had training and experience in learning how to make godly decisions. You can help him to gain that experience.

CHANGES IN THINKING

The changes that can take place in the thinking and decision mak-ing of a late adolescent allow him to move much closer to being a mature adult. We say *can* take place because these changes are not auto-matic. Exercising our mental "muscles" is similar to an athlete exercis-ing his physical muscles. If there is no exercise, little growth and development will take place. However, we hope that your son is getting a mental workout, gaining in the mental strength that will help him to think responsibly and make mature, adultlike decisions. If so, you can expect to see the following changes in how he thinks and looks at his world.

1. *He shows an increasing ability to think in the abstract.* For teens who have been encouraged to practice the mental abilities that they began to develop as middle adolescents, they should be getting better at analyzing situations. Abstract thinking allows your son to consider what should be, not just what is. He can be encouraged to think of different options and alternatives. Not all teens are encouraged to do so, and their lack of practice is reflected in immaturity.

   While this ability may be growing, it is unrealistic to assume that your son will use it all the time or in every decision. Studies have shown that teens (and adults, for that matter) apply this skill to some areas, but not others. For instance, your son may show real maturity in thinking about what he wants to do after high school graduation. He may systematically evaluate the advantages and disadvantages of going to college versus going to work, or he may research why he should go to one college over another. At the same time, you may see what you consider to be "airhead" decisions about what to do with his friends on a Friday night. If those decisions get him in trouble, you may hear "Sorry, dad, I just wasn't thinking." And he'll be right. You can encourage your children to use this ability to think in the abstract, but don't expect maturity and well-thought-out decisions in everything.

2. *He will be less self-conscious and concerned about an imaginary audience.* Remember that a middle adolescent becomes preoccupied with how others see him. He is concerned with an "imaginary audience," thinking that everything he does is seen and judged by others. This creates a lot of anxiety and pressure. As a late adolescent, he still has concerns about what others think, but their opinions exert far less pressure and anxiety at this stage than they did during middle adolescence.

   Growing mental skills allow boys ages sixteen to eighteen to do a better job of distinguishing between whose opinion is important and whose is not. They also become aware that much of their behavior goes unnoticed by the majority of their peers. As a result, older teens tend to be more comfortable with who they are, and their self-esteem is more stable.

3. *His thinking broadens to a wider range of topics.* The world of a junior high student, the early adolescent, is pretty narrow—who likes who, hanging out with friends, the pressures and activities of school, and

planning what to do this weekend. As we saw, midadolescents begin to apply their newfound ability to think abstractly to these and some other areas, but their concerns are generally limited to what is affecting their life. While late adolescents are equally concerned with the above issues, they also can become more aware and interested in things beyond their own personal world.

Famine in Africa, abortion protests, political events in Washington, and other current events may capture their attention more quickly than when they were younger. Thus broader social, political, and moral issues enter their thinking, and there is no longer a narrow focus on personal matters.

Now, you may be reading this thinking that Chap and I are living in a dream world. After all, the high school teens you know are nothing but a bunch of selfish, immature kids who only care about getting what they want and having a good time in life. Right?

The fact is that there are times when that's exactly what late adolescents are like. But there are other times when they can surprise you.

It's true that their interest in world issues and things that go beyond their own personal life may not be developed. In those cases, this thinking may need to be stimulated, but it can be done. Taking the time to gently nudge them toward the big questions of life, encouraging them to use that "thinker's permit," will often pay off in productive thinking.

4. *He is learning and improving in the ability to evaluate the perspective of others.* For the most part, late adolescents are gaining in what John Flavell calls a "sense of the game."[1] In order to play the "game" of life well, a man needs to learn how to read other people, evaluate alternatives, anticipate and solve problems, and relate to others in effective ways. Your boy is now entering that stage of evaluating information and others' opinions.

One of the marks of mature, adult thought is the ability to consider how others may look at a particular issue or decision. As your son grows in these skills, he will become better able to pick up on cues from others that help him to modify his behavior in socially acceptable ways. Thus, his relationships can deepen, becoming more mature than those he had in midadolescence. He often will be more realistic about his friendships.

The above four factors all combine to point up the need for late adolescents to be given opportunities to think and make decisions about life, themselves, and their relationships. They are not far from having to do that as full-fledged adults.

"Who Am I?"

Forging an Identity

Late adolescence is a time when teens are confronted with a number of identity issues. An older teen will ask himself at various times "Who Am I?" and healthy development requires that he defines who he is in several areas. Here are just six questions your son will be asking himself as he finishes his high school years:

1. What are my strengths and weaknesses?
2. What are my sexual values?
3. What qualities are important to me in friendships?
4. What do I believe about God?
5. Am I happy with how I'm doing in school?
6. What kind of work do I want to do as an adult?

All of these questions, together with many more, help to define a person's identity. Most researchers and theorists believe that adolescence, especially late adolescence, is the time in life when we first wrestle with these questions in a meaningful way.

Different teens handle these questions in different ways. Some tackle them in a serious way, while others simply ignore them. Researchers have discovered that how a teen deals with identity issues is related to the way that his family functions—that is, how your son deals with questions of identity will be determined in part by how you relate to him. So what are the ways your son can approach these questions of identity, and what role do you play in which way he goes?

Four Approaches to Identity

Most teens will approach questions about their identity in one of four ways. They can be avoiding, become settled, continue searching, or have achieved their self-interest, according to researcher James Marcia.[2] Let's study four eighteen-year-old boys becoming men, who have chosen different approaches in answering the question "Who am I?" Each reflects a type of thinking about one's personal identity.

1. *The avoiding type.* Jim is too concerned with today and doing things with his friends to think about who he is or what he wants to do with

his life. He figures that he'll just "go with the flow" and that eventually he'll fall into something he likes. Jim is clearly the avoiding type. He considers meetings with his high school counselor to discuss his plans for after graduation to be a real drag. Ask him about his plans, and he may say, "I don't really think about it. I like what's happening now, and that's what really matters." He says he has no goals, except to live for what he can get out of today.

Teens like Jim, who avoid dealing with questions of identity, often have low self-esteem and are often irresponsible. Their thinking is more childlike than adultlike. They live for themselves, and pleas from adults to grow up are met with indifference.

Avoiding teens tend to come from families that have distant or rejecting relationships. It is a negative atmosphere, and fathers of avoiding teens are often critical or absent. The lack of healthy family relationships seems to lead to an "I don't really care" attitude about life and goals.

2. *The settled type.* Casey seems to have all the answers when it comes to questions of identity. He's the settled type. He knows what he believes, what he wants to do with his life, and what his values are. The problem with Casey is that he's always known these things. You see, Casey has always been told what to believe and who he should be, and that's just the way it is. He has never considered being anything else. Rather than thinking about and deciding who he is and what he wants, he has simply adopted who his parents have told him to be.

Teens like Casey have no struggle when it comes to identity formation. They tend to seek the approval of others, especially parents. In a sense, they let other people do their thinking for them. They have all the questions answered, but they can get defensive when asked why they believe what they do. They are generally happy and have high self-esteem, although they are not very adaptable. Their relationship with parents is usually warm and loving, while at the same time the parents find direct and indirect ways to pressure them into accepting family values and beliefs.

3. *The searching type.* Joe has been having a lot of struggles thinking about his future. There are so many options, and he's not sure what direction he wants to take in life. Every time he thinks he gets questions about who he is and what he wants to do figured out, he talks himself out of it. He is the typical searching type.

Joe grew up in the church, and he admires the strong Christian commitment that his parents have. He accepted Christ in fourth-grade Sunday school, and his faith is important to him. Lately, though, he has had some doubts about his faith. Those doubts have led him to search out answers to his questions. He's gradually putting his thoughts and beliefs together, but it hasn't been easy.

Teens like Joe are searching. They wrestle with questions of identity and don't settle for easy answers or answers that are handed to them by others. Overall, they feel as if they can handle their world and that they are capable of finding answers to identity questions. They have good self-esteem, and their relationships with parents are positive and healthy. They tend to live in families that encourage children to take responsibility for their lives and to think for themselves. While parents want their children to adopt their values and lifestyle, they do not want to spoon-feed them the answers to life.

4. *The achieved type.* Terry is a confident, happy young adult who knows who he is and what he believes. Not long ago he was searching for answers, just like Joe. Terry spent a lot of time thinking about himself and God's plan for his life. Discussions with his father, pastor, and a close adult friend of the family helped him to sort out answers to his questions.

Teens like Terry have managed to develop a mature outlook on identity issues. They have invested a lot of thought into the important issues in their life. After carefully considering all the possibilities, they have made choices to which they are now committed. They are well-equipped to handle the situations that life brings their way.

Terry and others who have searched and believe they understand their identity are called achieved types. They have completed the struggle of deciding who they. They are settled and comfortable in their identity. Like the searching types, teens who are settled types come from families where love and care are blended with encouragement to be one's self.

Which of the above four types do you want your son to be, dad? We hope that you opt for the achieved type. Late adolescent boys (and girls) who become achieved types are the best prepared for handling the ups and downs that adulthood brings. They know who they are, and they know why. And you are a key player in helping them get there. Here are some ways you can help your son move to an achieved identity.

- Give him plenty of support and affection.
- Create a warm family climate that allows for healthy disagreement.
- Encourage him to think and talk about his future.

- Celebrate his ability to make decisions and be independent.
- Talk *with* him, not at him.
- Give him the freedom to be his own person, uniquely created by God.

As our children leave home and take their place in the world, we want them to go with a strong sense of identity that will help them to stand as committed men and women who know what it means to love and serve their God.

HELPING YOUR SON TO OWN HIS FAITH

Thinking through and learning to "own" their own faith in God is another crucial mental area that late teens develop. We can and must help our sons think through their faith. Shane, sixteen, has been bothered lately by doubts about his Christian faith. His active witness in school has prompted a number of guys to start asking him questions— questions that he has a hard time answering. "How do you know the Bible is from God? If God is so loving, why is there so much suffering and evil in the world? Wasn't Jesus just a great teacher? How do you know he was God and that he rose from the dead?" These and other questions have been getting to Shane, making him wonder why he believes what he does.

The more Shane thought about it, the more he realized that he didn't know why he believed what he did. He had grown up with answers that worked for him, but those answers did not satisfy his skeptical friends. At first he tried to shrug off his doubts, but they kept coming back. "What if I'm wrong? What if my parents and my church are wrong? How do I know that Christianity is the only way to heaven?" He needed to find out.

He was afraid to go to his dad. He considered Dad so sure of himself —strong, committed, faithful—and Shane didn't know how to approach him. But Shane wanted to be strong, too, and eventually those nagging doubts drove him to seek advice from his father. Unfortunately, Dad responded to Shane's questions and doubts with anger and defensiveness. Rather than discussing them with his son, Dad told Shane to just have faith and resist Satan's attempts to get him to doubt. With no discussion and no answers, he left Shane to feel guilty for doubting.

Too many parents underestimate the importance of helping their teenagers to think through their faith. Our sons need to own their faith for themselves, and coming to grips with doubts and questions is a necessary step to ownership. Their questions and doubts cannot be answered by indoctrination or spoon-feeding. If we tell them what to believe, it is our beliefs that are held, not theirs. We must help them to discover faith for themselves, not for us.

Granting our sons the freedom to explore questions of faith can be a scary proposition. After all, they may not end up where we want them to go. The truth is, however, that we cannot force our sons to believe what we want them to believe. Spiritual guidance in late adolescence is best handled by helping them to think about their faith, not by trying to limit their questions. Tom Bisset, author of *Why Christian Kids Leave the Faith,* states, "In my interviews with faith dropouts, nothing evoked stronger reactions than the simple question, 'Did you feel free to make important decisions about your faith at home and in church?'"[3] We must realize that if we try to force our son to believe, and if we squash his questions, we may drive him away from a faith commitment.

The questions that our sons ask need to be celebrated, not feared. They are thinking about vital questions, as they should, in order to become independent—and in the case of spiritual matters, assured about their faith. As we work with our sons rather than against them to answer those questions, their faith grows and plants itself deeper in our sons' souls. As Bisset suggests,

> We must also ask ourselves why Christians are so unwilling to grant others spiritual freedom, particularly their own children. If an intelligent visitor from another planet were to contemplate the myriad rules and regulations that are part and parcel of most evangelical homes and churches, he or she might well conclude that in these places, freedom is the enemy. This observer might also infer that the right to make an authentic choice in matters of faith is among the most dangerous of all possibilities.[4]

Talk with your son. Discuss questions of faith. Debate issues with him. Help him to think—don't think for him. In giving him the freedom to think for himself, you maximize the chances that that he will invite you to share in that process with him. As you think together with him, call him to a knowledge of the Scriptures. Encourage him to search out the answers to his doubts and questions in God's Word. They are there for him to discover.

The road to an achieved identity that is grounded in a solid faith relationship with Jesus Christ must be travelled by our son. We cannot travel it for him, but we can walk alongside him as he searches for a mature faith that is reasoned as well as childlike.

TWELVE
SOCIAL CURVES

You're almost there! Your son is rapidly approaching the launch pad to adulthood. You can almost hear the countdown. Blastoff from home is too close. In only a couple of years that little boy you used to burp is a full-fledged adult. How many parents haven't made remarks like "It seems only yesterday he . . ." But he is not there yet. He still needs you as he continues to develop socially. There are dangerous curves ahead, where you can help him mature.

In the life of a busy teenager, spending time can be a problem. In fact, finding him can be a problem. But the reality is that late adolescents are home more often than it seems. A clever experiment by Mihaly Czikszentmihalyi and Reed Larson has given us some insight into how high school students spend their time and who they spend it with.[1]

In the study, seventy-five students were given beepers to carry with them wherever they went. The beepers would sound at random approximately every two hours that the teens were awake. The students then recorded where they were when the beeper sounded, what they were doing, and who they were with. The results of their study are summarized in two revealing pie charts (see next page).

As you can see, home is where teens spend much of their time. But when it comes to who they are with, teens spend a lot of time with their peer group. More than half of their waking time is spent with other teenagers, while only 20 percent of their time is with their family (and very little of that time with parents only). Clearly much of their time at home is spent sleeping and eating (any surprises there?) and a much lesser amount interacting with family members.

TEENS AND THEIR TIMES

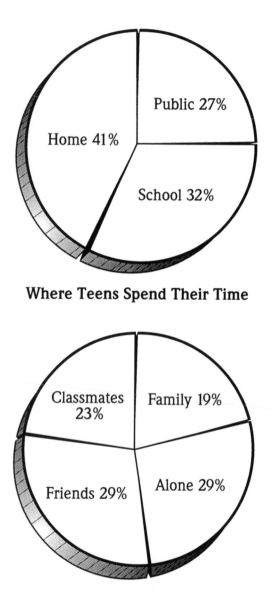

Where Teens Spend Their Time

Who Teens Spend Their Time With

Source: Adapted from Mihaly Csikszentmihalyi & Reed Larson,
Being Adolescent: Conflict and Growth in the Teenage Years
(New York: Basic, 1984), 59, 63.

The teens in this study reported that they were happiest when they were with their friends, but being with their family ranked second. The reason for this, at least in part, is that they have more fun with friends than family. Joking, laughing, and just goofing off are more common with friends than family.[2] Builds a strong case for family fun, huh?

RELATIONSHIPS WITH PEERS: CHOOSING A GROUP

As the above study confirms, being with friends is an important part of late adolescence. But the intense need to conform and be accepted by the entire peer group lessens to some extent. There is less concern with being liked by everyone—that concern extends only to one's immediate circle of friends. While we saw that midadolescents are intensely concerned with asking the question "Do you like me?", late adolescents are more likely to ask the question "Do I like you?" Fears and insecurities are still present, but late adolescents have reached a point where they have a much better sense of identity. They have discovered in part who they are and who they want their friends to be.

Walk into a high school cafeteria at lunchtime. Although you won't be able to see them, invisible boundaries mark out who can sit where—and all the students know where those boundaries are. In one corner, you'll see a bunch of athletes, at another table a group of so-called nerds, and back in one corner a gang of alienated teens who live for drugs and delinquency. You'll also see large groups of average teens who are known for nothing in particular, but they achieve well in school and stay out of trouble. You'll notice a lot of activity as you scan these groups—eating, talking, teasing, flirting, and just goofing off. In all this activity, it is apparent that there is little interaction between certain groups. The lines of friendship have been set. Different groups have different standards of behavior. Being accepted looks different, depending on your circle of friends.

In the context of this circle of friends, there is one thing that captures a lot of your son's attention. No, it's not homework, or helping at home, or scraping the bubble gum off the bottom of desks as a volunteer service project. It's girls. The interest that started in midadolescence continues to occupy a strong place in his thinking, and sometimes in his behavior.

RELATIONSHIPS WITH THE OPPOSITE SEX

Compared to midadolescence, dating in this stage is much more couple-oriented. Relationships become more serious, and they also are based in a stronger level of maturity than junior high romances. How-ever, there is still a lot to be learned. This growing maturity, combined with trial-and-error learning, gives rise to questions about dating that are more relational than those asked by the junior highers. Here are three you are likely to encounter from your older teenage boy:

Is it all right to date several girls at once?

How can you tell if you're really in love?

How can you break up without hurting the other person?[3]

We need to be available to help our teens answer such questions. Dating can be an important part of our son's development, but we still need to encourage him to keep his social world large enough to include many friends and dates. When teens lock themselves into an exclusive relationship that consumes all of their time, they cheat themselves out of a rich, satisfying social life. Furthermore, when that relationship narrows, his world can become isolated and too "me" or "us" focused with the opposite sex. A couple who isolate themselves from a wide base of friends increase the temptation and risk of a powerful force in a late adolescent—sexuality.

Those wonderful curves that God in His infinite wisdom created for women do not escape the notice of your son. Thinking about girls is a frequent subject in your son's mind—more frequent than you might imagine.

This preoccupation with girls can result in a great deal of sexual temptation for your son, either mentally or behaviorally. That preoccu-pation is almost encouraged in the nineties, when teenage boys are bombarded by sexual messages that fly in the face of God's standards. Movies, television sitcoms, music, MTV, and magazines all send the message that being sexually active as a teenager is normal. Even sex education experts have bought this standard. Abstinence is given lip service, but the real sex education message is to do what you want, just be safe.

A young man recently spoke up in a discussion of sexuality at a small Christian college. "I don't want to seem like a prude or anything, but the Bible clearly teaches that sex before marriage is sin." The pres-sure to live a godly lifestyle without appearing "uncool" is real. Even at a Christian college he felt compelled to explain his position to fellow Christians. Every teen is hearing a message that sex before marriage, as long as you love each other and take proper precautions, is OK. And many teens, including Christian teens, are giving in to that message.

SOCIAL CURVES

In his revealing study "Premarital Sex: Attitudes and Behavior by Dating Stage," researcher John Roche reported on teenage sexual behaviors. He asked teens about sexual behavior: what they did, what kinds of sexual behaviors they thought were proper, and what sexual behaviors they thought other teens were doing at different stages of dating. Among his more significant findings were: (1) boys expect physical intimacy at earlier dating stages than girls, (2) teens reported that they were engaged in sexual behaviors that they said were not proper, (3) intimate sexual behavior increased for stages of dating that included love or commitment, and (4) teens believed that their peers were more sexually active than what those peers reported.[4]

It is generally agreed that, at least in terms of their behavior, Christian youth are not very far behind non-Christian youth in their level of sexual activity. Youth pastors and others who work with our teens are well aware of the sexual involvement that is going on, and often tell sad stories of Christian teens in sexual struggles and failures at national youth conferences. According to Josh McDowell, a popular Christian author and speaker, "Statistics show the figure [of sexually active teens] to be between 65 and 80 percent depending on the statistics one chooses. Surprisingly, Christian teenagers are generally only ten percentage points or so behind the overall figure."[5]

So what does all of this mean for your growing son? For one thing, he is not immune to the pressures and cultural messages that push kids into early sexual behavior. You also should realize that the values he holds are no guarantee that he will not find himself caught in ways that he knows are wrong.

Helping your son deal with his sexuality is important, and many good books and resources are available to help Christian parents to do this. You can also help by letting him know that everyone else is not doing it, in spite of what teens often think or hear from some friends. In addition to our instructions, our sons need to know that we love them no matter what, and that we want them to be able to bring their questions and concerns about anything to us, including dating and sexuality.

As we have already seen, much of this pressure is coming at a time when your son is spending more time with peers than with anyone else. Time with parents is more limited, but that doesn't mean the time is insignificant.

Relationship with Parents

During late adolescence, strong conflict emerges between the parent and child; or if conflict has occurred earlier, this is a time when it deepens. Your sons (and daughters) are seeking independence and identity, and they will test and stretch you even more, even if they are children who follow Christ. Consider Rick, a typical late adolescent from a good Christian family. He has grown up in the church, accepted Christ at camp when he was ten years old, and has been an active member of his church youth group throughout his teenage years.

Most of his friends at school, including his girlfriend, are good kids from Christian homes. Rick loves to spend time with his friends—going to games, movies, and just hanging out at each other's houses. He enjoys the time that he spends with his family, and they have always been close. But given a choice between spending time with dad, mom, and little brother or spending time with friends, friends win hands down. His busy social life, combined with his part-time job and schoolwork, doesn't leave much family time. Home seems more like a bed and breakfast than a home. Dad and mom want that to change.

An Ultimatum

Wanting to spend more time with Rick, Dad puts his foot down. "Rick, you're just not home much anymore, and that has to change. I want you to drop something so that you can be home more—give us time to do things together." Rick is not unsympathetic, but he loves all his activities and time spent with friends—he doesn't want to miss out on anything.

"Dad, I'll try to be home more, but I just don't want to drop anything I'm in right now."

"Rick," Dad replies, "I'm not asking you to drop something, I'm telling you. End of discussion."

Over the next few weeks, Rick starts to dig his heels in, making excuses and refusing to cut back on his activity. His relationship with his dad becomes strained, and arguments start to flare.

Who's right, and who's wrong? Who would you rather defend—Rick or his dad? Dad's request for a little more time spent at home with family is certainly a reasonable desire, isn't it? But isn't it normal for a teenager to want to spend time with his friends, not wanting to miss out on any of the "cool" experiences that happen in their lives? Something needs to give somewhere.

Conflicts between parents and late adolescents are not uncommon. In fact, conflicts in close relationships are inevitable—you can't achieve intimacy without having some conflict. The problem is not the conflict, but what you do with it. Conflict is an opportunity to grow and develop if it is handled the right way.

Types of Arguments

So what do parents and teens fight and argue about? We mentioned in chapter 7 that conflicts tend to be over social issues, not major values. F. Philip Rice has examined the studies that deal with parent-teen conflicts, and he discovered that these conflicts tend to fall into four categories.[6] How many of the following sources of conflict have you run into with your son?

1. *His social life.* This includes his choices for friends or dating partners and the amount of time he spends with friends or dates. Another point of social debate is his choice of hairstyles or clothing.

2. *His responsibility.* This includes his performance of household chores and how he spends money. Two other areas are the use of the family car and telephone time.

3. *His school performance.* His performance in classes and grades can become an issue of debate. Study habits and completion of homework also can lead to arguments.

4. *Family Relationships.* For some older teenagers, conflicts come when they physically or verbally fight with brothers or sisters. For others, their attitudes and level of respect shown to parents can bring conflict.

Whichever ones look familiar, isn't it nice to know that you're not alone? Conflict with a teenager will happen at least occasionally, so be prepared. The goal is to resolve the conflict without damaging the relationship.

As we have seen before, parents of a well-adjusted teen gradually give him more and more freedom to run his own life and make his own decisions. It's appropriate to treat your son as he would like to be treated —as someone who's becoming a responsible and respected adult. You should move from parental power toward shared power. Discussion and negotiation, not commands, are the tools for resolving problems and conflicts.

So parents have no control or veto power—is that what we're saying? Not at all. While there is change, and even reduction, in parental power as children grow to adulthood, parents are never without influence. At no stage do teens in healthy families perceive power to be equal, and surprisingly, they don't think it should be either. God has given us responsibility for the godly training of our children, and even our children recognize that. But that does not mean they will willingly cooperate with whatever methods we choose to do that training.

Responsible, godly parents do not throw out guidelines and standards and abandon their teens. Some standards are not negotiable—drugs, premarital sex, etc. But even in those cases, we cannot command our teens to obey. We must be clear about our values and expectations, but we are more likely to impact our teenage children and gain their cooperation when we participate in discussions rather than command them.

So what happened with Rick and his dad? Dad's intentions were good, but handing down an ultimatum to a late adolescent is like throwing fuel on a fire. It's going to blow up. Even if Rick had been inclined to work something out, dad's ultimatum most likely insured his resistance. Teenagers—and adults for that matter—don't like to be squashed with power. If Rick and his dad would have taken the time to sit and discuss their desires and tensions, the chances are high that they could have worked something out. And in doing that, Rick would have had the opportunity to add to his skills in making good decisions and resolving conflict in a healthy way.

THE ROAD TO INDEPENDENCE

Remember, our sons are marching down the road toward independence. We need to encourage them to walk that road and be willing to walk alongside them. Late adolescents who are able to achieve a solid sense of autonomy are more self-confident and mature than those who do not.

Some teens see their parents as roadblocks to independence. They believe that the primary task they have as a teenager is to break free from their parents. It does not have to be that way, but that depends on the parents.

Separateness and connectedness are not opposites. You do not need to give up one in order to have the other. Even if you are spending less time with your son by his choice, the connection can remain strong. In fact, the presence of warm, healthy connections between a father and his son can provide the foundation for growth in autonomy. Studies of successful teenagers confirm this fact. "Traditional thinking about adolescents' needs for growing separation and independence from their parents is giving way to the conception that teens grow more competent and self-directed through a renegotiated interdependence with parents. . . . In general, healthy development is increasingly seen as happening in a context where both autonomy and attachment and connection with parents are highly valued."[7]

Healthy independence is based in a secure sense of belonging, not isolation. Mature teens who successfully forge an independent identity usually report feelings of closeness to their parents. While closeness brings occasional conflict, it also brings a lot of satisfaction.

THE WORLD OF WORK

A new social world opens to the late adolescent: work. Late adolescence is a time when many teens get their first real job. The attraction of earning their own money, and more of it than dad or mom is usually willing to give, can be a powerful motivator. The novelty, lessons, and even fun that come with cooking food and actually using the words "sir" or "ma'am" in a sentence make employment look like a great idea. In fact, many teens have a simple way of looking at work for pay: "Adults hold down jobs, so having your first real job is a mark of moving to adulthood. Right?"

Recognize that should your son (or daughter) enter the workplace as a part-time worker, he will receive a number of benefits but also will encounter some drawbacks. He will learn responsibility. Whether it is working in a fast-food restaurant, landscaping for a lawn service, bagging groceries, or any number of other jobs teens are usually able to get, he will learn about punctuality, how to follow the instructions of an employer, and how to work with other employees as a team. And he gets paid along with learning these valuable character traits! Given these benefits, it would seem like a good idea for all late adolescents to go out and get a job. Or is it such a good idea?

Researchers who have studied the effects of employment have discovered that the wonderful world of work has its drawbacks for teenagers. Many teens who work part time are less involved in school, and their grades often suffer. They may focus more on cutting ties with their parents, and they spend less time in family activities.[8] These problems connected with working are especially likely for those who work more than fifteen hours per week. In fact, it seems as if the major, and only, advantage that working teens have over nonworking teens is the money that they earn.

These results suggest two things. First, adding a part-time job to the busy life of a teenager will reduce what is an already small amount of time with family. The healthy development of an independent teenager requires a connectedness with parents, but staying in contact is difficult when parents and children rarely see each other. Second, developing character traits such as punctuality and being a team player in your children can be done in many ways besides having a job. Many students gain similar qualities through participation in extracurricular activities at school, leadership positions in their church youth group, or other organized activities. Speech, music, drama, athletics, clubs, and other opportunities can all teach responsibility and character development. And students involved in these types of activities do not tend to have the kinds of problems that were described above for those teens who work.

Whether or not your son should take a part-time job, especially during the school year, is a decision that you should talk about together. Let's look at how two families handled this issue.

Mark and his son, Josh, sat down to talk one evening after supper. Mark listened a long time as Josh talked about why he wanted to get a job. Though Josh talked about the skills that he would learn from having a job, it was also clear that the major motivation was money. Josh was thrilled with the prospect of earning enough money to keep himself in new clothes, and he was especially excited about the chance to earn enough to buy a car (on monthly payments, that is).

"You'd have to give up several things if you took a job," his father answered. "Time with friends, time with family, activities at school, free Saturdays, and a few other things. Have you thought much about that?"

"Well, I guess that's true. It's not that I want to give those things up. I really don't want to. But I don't see other choices. I mean, I need to earn some money, Dad."

As Josh and his dad talked some more they finally came up with a solution that made both of them happy. Mark decided to become Josh's employer. In addition to regular chores around the house, Josh was now hired to do more major tasks. For example, Josh was given the responsibility of painting the house. Mark worked with him, which gave him the opportunity to teach him some valuable skills. Josh was able to earn the money he wanted, and he received the added benefit of special times with his dad. As Josh would finish each job, they would negotiate for a new one. They both got what they wanted, and their relationship grew as well.

Paul and his son, Joe, took a different approach. Joe wanted to pick up a part-time job in order to save for Christmas gifts and some extra clothes. He had some interest in a sales career, and he thought that a job in the local department store would give him some experience and skills to get that career started.

Paul listened carefully to Joe, then discussed the matter with his wife. After carefully thinking and praying about it, they decided that taking the job could be a good experience for Joe. Joe's motive was right—the money was for others as well as himself, and the job could give him important skills. Their consent was not without some strings attached, though. Joe sat down with his parents, and soon they had negotiated some guidelines that they all were happy with.

Like Paul, you should work out some guidelines about a part-time job as long as your son is in school and living at home. Here are seven to consider as you talk with your son:

1. Before saying yes to your son, be sure that your wife agrees with you about his working. If she does not, discover her objections, including her in the discussion you have with your son.

2. The job cannot interfere with his ability to complete his homework and maintain his grades.

3. You and your son must agree on a maximum number of hours. (We recommend no more than ten hours per week).

4. The job cannot interfere with church activities or youth group on a regular basis.

5. His work cannot become a source of family tension or conflict.

6. A portion of his income needs to be set aside for tithing and saving.

7. Agree on a trial period (three months, for example), after which time you and your son will review the merits of his job.

The issue of working can be handled in a number of ways. However you choose to negotiate this area of your son's life, one thing is important: do not simply hand your son money to satisfy his financial wants. He has reached a point where he is becoming a man, and the connection between income and responsibility is a necessary lesson of adult life.

THIRTEEN
THE LATE ADOLESCENT PLAYBOOK

Though your boy will always be your son, these are the final years you have to significantly influence and mold him as he becomes a man. In most cases, once he leaves home for college, work, or the military, the job of parenting is over. Sure, you may still have some leverage in his decision making, and you may have a bit of control over his money, but, for the most part, he will be on his own.

So what is the goal of this last phase of adolescence, this closing season of childhood? To encourage your son to practice being a man while still maintaining the relative safety net of home and family, with all the security that brings.

When I (Chap) was a junior in high school, barely seventeen, I asked my parents if I could borrow their car and drive to Lake Tahoe from San Jose, California, to go skiing with two friends for the weekend. One friend's family owned a small cabin on the lake, and I had driven in snow once before, so I felt somewhat prepared for the weekend adventure. I wasn't so sure, however, if my parents felt the same way. To my great surprise they were all for it—no fuss, no argument, just, "Drive safely" and "Have a good time!"

This was one of the greatest gifts my parents gave me prior to sending me off to college a year and a half later. I not only went into the weekend with the blessing (and even encouragement) of my folks, but with the knowledge that if they believed that I could handle such a trip, then surely they were right! Their confidence and trust instilled in me a confidence and trust in myself. To this day I feel a sense of pride and security in planning and implementing any type of travel. That weekend in high school helped me to believe in myself as an adult worthy of responsibility.

This is the key to rites of passage in the late adolescent stage of development—instilling in your son the confidence that he is capable of responsibility and trust. You are preparing your child-almost-adult to believe that he is able to handle even the unexpected and difficult situations that responsibility brings and to help him feel worthy of trust. Hopefully you have been giving your son lots of opportunities to learn responsibility and demonstrate that he can be trusted. He is coming into the home stretch, and the finish line of adulthood is not far away. The building of trust and responsibility is now ready for the finishing touches.

Whether he is dealing with the logistics of daily tasks (such as getting to places on time, handling rest and nutrition needs, or meeting a budget), going on a short trip, handling his sexual drive, or dealing with social relationships, now is not the time for a father to clamp down. It is the time to let go, with the assurance you will stay by his side when he needs you. It is too early to give him complete and total freedom from authority, of course, but it is also too late for control and restraint.

More than ever, then, rites of passage are helpful during these years in that they communicate continued movement from boyhood toward becoming a man. With each rite communicated, anticipated, and realized comes a new awareness of the healthy sense of autonomy that manhood brings.

Training for Integrity

It is equally crucial, however, to underscore every privilege and opportunity with the need for your son to show integrity. Without a commitment to integrity, freedom becomes an expression of self-interest and deceit. Truth, authenticity, openness, and accountability must be hammered home at this final stage of adolescence, or your son may fall prey to the cultural temptation to take the easy road whenever possible.

What marks the difference between the man of integrity and the man who takes shortcuts in life? The man without integrity cheats on his taxes, drives with a radar detector (sorry, fellas, but there is only one purpose for such a device—to get away with breaking the law), lusts after other men's wives, lies to clients, and pads his expense account, often blaming the government for his financial situation. He will try to justify his deceit. In contrast, the man of integrity honors and cherishes his wife above all others, is grateful for and wise with the money he has, pays his parking tickets, is happier, has a healthier marriage, and possesses the kind of character that God can use. This is what you should desire for your son.

If you give your son more and more freedom, he has more chances for failure, compromise, and even painful consequences. This is a period when your son, still learning, may make wrong choices. He may fail at times. But a far greater danger at this stage is to create an environment where your son cannot be honest in the midst of failure and struggle. Should he fail, you still must communicate acceptance. If you communicate love, honor, and respect only when he is doing well, he may feel forced to hide his dirt from you, eventually driving himself deeper into deceit. If as fathers we let our sons know that we believe in them, even when they fail, and we are willing to help walk them through the consequences of failure (not rescuing, but advising and caring for them), we are helping them to see that there is far greater freedom and joy in honest living. Building a man of integrity means granting him the freedom to fail without forcing him to "go underground."

RITES OF PASSAGE FOR LATE ADOLESCENTS

These ideas and suggestions, then, are meant to fit this unique stage of adolescence. As in chapters 7 and 10, they are not exhaustive, nor should you try to do them all. Pick a few that work for you, and be flexible so that your son doesn't feel forced or coerced. For each rite of passage to be most effective, make sure it is anticipated, preferably by the entire family, and carries significant, shared meaning. These ideas are fun, they are memorable, and we trust that you will find them helpful on your journey of taking your son the last few steps toward manhood.

Family Plays

1. *Let him plan most vacations.* It's time to maximize his responsibilities now, so give your son the responsibility for planning vacation logistics. Devise with him a planning sheet for handling all of the details of one major family vacation. Get him to secure family input, obtain the necessary maps and brochures, and get the car gassed and serviced for the trip.

2. *Make him an alternate driver.* Maybe during vacation trips you do all the driving; maybe your wife is the second driver who spells you on a long road trip. Either way, it's time for an alternate driver. Let him drive on vacation.

3. *Ask him to lead family devotions on a regular basis.* It may be once a week or once a month.

4. *Have him plan and lead a family service opportunity.*

School Plays

1. *Hold an academic conference.* Have him set a specific timetable for his future after high school graduation. Ask him to outline what the important factors in making the decision are. Decide with him options for the future, especially as it relates to college finances and grades. Perhaps he will choose to work, so negotiate with him how his role at home will change. To make this a rite of passage, this should be arranged on a timetable so that you will maintain anticipation, and can help him to see the value of planning for his future.

2. *Leave a school legacy.* By the end of the summer before his senior year have him define what legacy he wants to leave at school. Ask him to write a paragraph of what he would like others to say about him after he has graduated. Help him to devise goals for the year based on this legacy.

3. *Have him target his school.* Encourage your son to create a plan for evangelism for the final few years at school. One idea is an evangelistic technique called "the points of the compass." The strategy has him identifying one class per semester where he will focus. When he gets into class, he identifies the four "points of the compass," the person in front of, behind, and next to him on either side. During the semester he regularly prays for them, gets to know them, tangibly cares for them, and prays for the opportunity to share Christ with each of them, possibly through a Christian group on campus or your church.

4. *Make a friend.* Help your son to recognize that as Christians we are called to love the unlovely. Ask him to identify one person per year to befriend and love, simply because Jesus loves them. The kind of person he chooses may be one who has no friends, or who is clearly different from his comfortable crowd (perhaps racially, socially, or physically). Help your son to realize that we each have a great deal to learn from those who are different, and we can grow in our understanding of the bigness of our God through these types of relationships.

Social Plays

1. *Have him take a weekend trip without his family.* During his senior year of high school, let him take a short trip with a friend or two for a weekend. Make sure you do not give more freedom than is warranted by your son, his friends, and the trip itself (maybe not a trip to Ft. Lauderdale over spring break, for example). Help him to decide on a trip that is appropriate for him, and walk with him through the planning stages.

2. *Encourage deep friendships outside the family.* Every year, encourage your son to identify three to five people whom he can commit to developing deep, accountable relationships. Better yet, help him to include a few girls in this tight circle of friends. Though cliques have gotten bad press over the years, learning how to develop intimate friendships with members of both sexes is very important in becoming a man of integrity and depth.

3. *Help him to start a support group of Christian friends* (or even an outreach group) from school. Help him to find tools and resources which can facilitate discussions that help them grow in their faith. (A local youth pastor or youth parachurch office can help here.)

4. *Promote a group dating club.* If your son is dating, encourage him to create a "group dating club" that builds friendships instead of excludes so many kids.

INTERIOR PLAYS

1. *Attend a retreat together.* Make a commitment to attend (or create) some sort of silent and/or directed retreat together four times a year. Before each retreat, agree together on some preparatory reading, and a theme for the time. Immediately afterward, discuss together what happened during the experience, and what conclusions, if any, were reached. Pray together both before and after the event.

2. *Send him on a solo retreat.* On a solitary weekend retreat your son can think about and reflect on his faith, values, and goals. Give him some questions to consider, and ask him to write down his responses to them. Suggest to him that he devote his time to digging deep into the Scriptures, praying with intensity, and listening to God. At the end of the weekend, meet him at a designated location where you can talk about what he learned. Have him share his reflections on the questions you give him to answer. Close your time by presenting him with some gift that signifies his entry into manhood. Return home for a family celebration!

3. *Hold a home conference.* Teachers evaluate students at school; parents can help evaluate and encourage their children at home. At regular intervals set up "evaluation" meetings between you and your son, or among your wife, you, and your son. Most people deeply fear the thought of honest evaluation, yet training your son to learn how to accept and (ultimately) gratefully acknowledge specific praise as well as constructive and loving criticism will be a tremendous gift to him as a man. The man who has enough strength of character to desire input into his life cannot help but become a man of great integrity.

By the way, this will be a futile, even potentially destructive, exercise if it is not mutual. Give your son the same invitation to give honest feeeback on how you're doing as father and leader. His comments can help in shaping your life as his dad as well.

4. *Get in the loop.* Much is happening outside the home, as we noted in chapter 10, and you need to be in that loop. Be in the know as to what's happening—not to be nosy but to rejoice in his successes and console him in his setbacks. Ask permission to debrief significant events with him. Here are a few: his first date with a new flame, a team tryout, finals week, a youth group retreat, and the class prom. By doing this you invite him to live a life of thoughtful reflection, instead of floating from one event to another.

5. *Become accountability partners.* Schedule weekly or bi-weekly meetings together where you can share your personal victories, fears, and temptations. Pray for each other, both during and between meetings. Hold each other mutually accountable for the things you each need to work on in your lives. This ritual is a man-to-man, friend-to-friend relationship—no room for parenting here. While your son still needs you as a parent, those times are hopefully becoming more limited as he demonstrates adultlike decision making and maturity.

FAITH PLAYS

1. *Encourage him to teach a Sunday school class.* Ask him to go over lesson plans with you, focusing on the solemnity of representing Jesus Christ with younger people. Debrief the experience afterward, especially helping him to see how God chose to work and move in the classroom.

2. *Take a spiritual gift inventory instrument together* (a very helpful tool of this type is the S.H.A.P.E. inventory designed by Rick Warren at Saddleback Church.[1]) After completing the inventory, discuss the findings. Discuss also with your son how God has gifted him and how God may be inviting him to service in the Kingdom.

3. *Do Bible studies together on issues* that specifically deal with areas that affect him. Topics could include: what it means to be a man of God, sexuality, integrity, relationships, the poor and oppressed, and the Christian's role in a pagan world.

4. *Develop a faith notebook.* As often as possible, attend worship services together and ask him to take notes on the sermon (even if this is not a common practice in your church). Get your son to maintain a "faith notebook" of sermons, Bible studies, talks, and other input that can be valuable in faith formation. A helpful strategy is to encourage him to look up scriptural passages for himself following a lesson or talk, and see if, in fact, the text said what the speaker claimed (this is not to make your son cynical or arrogant, but to let him know that a responsible man of God must seek the truth for himself, and not simply blindly follow the "experts"). Ask him to share with your family what he has learned about God and faith in doing such an exercise.

PART THREE
A FAITHFUL FATHER

A righteous man who walks in his integrity—
how blessed are his sons after him.

Proverbs 20:7 (NASB)

FOURTEEN
THE GREAT IMPRESSION

Writing in *What Makes a Man?* Fran Sciacca speaks to the real issue of turning boys into men when he says we fathers must "find out what our own hearts beat for."[1] The starting place for helping our boys to become men is not with our sons—it is with us. Who we are as men will make a difference in who our son becomes.

A Tale of Two Fathers

How much of an impact can one man make on his children and the generations of children that come after him? Let's compare the lives of two very different men—Jonathan Edwards and Max Jukes.[2]

The Legacy of Jonathan Edwards
You may have heard of Jonathan Edwards, a godly man some consider to be one of the most brilliant theologians in American history. Edwards lived in the 1700s, spending most of his adult life as a pastor. His faith was the foundation of his life, and that foundation was passed on to his children. He raised his children to love God, and he modeled his faith for them to see. There was no question in the minds of his children who Jonathan Edwards was—a passionate man of God, committed to teaching his children how to live by showing them his life.

Jonathan Edwards's example for his children powerfully shaped their character. And they became leaders, not because of innate giftedness or some great heritage that must be expressed, but because their father by word and deed instilled values of integrity and service in their lives. He left his mark on them. Of the generations that followed him, Jonathan's posterity reads like a Who's Who in America—one vice-president, senators, ambassadors, thirteen university presidents, sixty-five college professors, thirty-two noted authors, sixty prominent lawyers, ninety physicians, two hundred ministers, and more than three hundred successful farmers.

The Legacy of Max Jukes

Max Jukes lived at approximately the same time as Jonathan Edwards. You have probably not heard of Max. Little is known about him really, except that he was often in trouble. Max provided a model for his children that was very different, but just as powerful.

The impact of Jukes's modeling showed itself in his posterity—three hundred delinquents, one hundred forty-five drunkards, ninety prostitutes, one hundred who spent an average of thirteen years each in prison, and many more who died prematurely from accidents and diseases brought about by their lifestyle.

The generations that followed Jukes cost the state of New York millions of dollars. The generations that followed Jonathan Edwards made contributions to society that cannot be measured in dollars. A father's example reaches far into the future.

BEING A ROLE MODEL

Our society is in desperate need of fathers who will step up and be a model of strong character and integrity for their sons. Sadly, many boys are growing up with fathers who are absent, either emotionally or physically.

To fill the gap left by an absent father, boys resort to selecting other men as models. We all need someone to look up to. Typically boys choose television and sports heroes as their models. Not all of these heroes are flattered. All-star basketball player Charles Barkley spoke with bluntness but also wisdom when he said, "I have a sneaker deal myself, but I don't understand why people would buy one sneaker endorsed by one player over the other. Kids idolize professional athletes, which is wrong in itself, and they just copy what they're wearing. I think one of the problems we have in today's society is that it's the parents' job to be role models. To kids that idolize me, I tell them don't do so just because I can dribble a basketball—that's really sick."[3]

Barkley is right. Such heroes are only an image, not reality. Heroes cannot provide the model that shows boys what it means to be a man in everyday life. That takes you, dad. Are you up to the challenge? The life you lead is not only important to your son, it is important to God. A man who lives his faith in front of his family and the world is respected by others and honored by God.

The rural Indiana church was packed, and the overflow of people began to fill a fellowship hall where planners had wisely placed a large screen for a closed-circuit telecast of the event, a funeral. Ron Goetz—a husband, father of four, and friend to many—had fought an up-and-down battle with cancer for almost twelve years. God had now taken him home.

His son made his way to the pulpit at the front of the church. "Thank you for coming," he said. "This funeral service was planned and written by my father. . . ." The service reflected the man. It was a celebration—a homegoing celebration. Many listeners who knew Ron could picture him now standing by the side of his Savior, watching as his well-crafted service helped us all to celebrate the new life that he was enjoying.

As I (Steve) watched and listened to Ron, Jr., speak about his father, my mind went back to the days when Ron's son was a college student. Now he spoke proudly about the godly walk and influence of this man—his dad—whom he was now honoring.

God had used Ron in so many ways to touch hundreds of lives through the years, but perhaps most importantly Ron had touched the life of his son. He left him a legacy of spiritual enthusiasm and a model of what it means to walk with one's God.

Our world is in desperate need of men like Jonathan Edwards and Ron Goetz. God is waiting to empower you to be the primary spiritual model in your son's life.

A BIBLICAL CALL

One of the most significant calls to be a model for our sons is found in the history of the Jewish people—but it is a call that still resounds loudly for fathers today.

The Israelites were suffering in captivity, ruled by the oppressive hand of the Pharaoh of Egypt. God had promised to deliver them, but it seemed as if the deliverer would never come. For more than four hundred years they had waited and hoped, but still no deliverance.

But God always keeps his promises. Moses was called to deliver God's people in a miraculous way, and the days of their captivity came to an end. They were heading for the Promised Land, the land God had given to them through their ancestors. Though they suffered through a forty-year detour of wandering in the desert for disobeying and forsaking their God, the Israelites finally came to the bank of the Jordan River. Across the river lay the Promised Land, the land of freedom, flowing with milk and honey. Five centuries of waiting were coming to an end —they were ready to go into the land that God had promised to them and possess it.

After five centuries of waiting, we can assume that God's instructions to them on that momentous occasion would be particularly significant. He would now speak the words that they would carry with them into that land. This was a new beginning, and His deepest desire for His people would be captured in what was said to them that day. This is what the Lord their God said to them through Moses:

> These are the commands, decrees and laws the Lord your God directed me to teach you to observe in the land that you are crossing the Jordan to possess, so that you, your children and their children after them may fear the Lord your God as long as you live by keeping all his decrees and commands that I give you, and so that you may enjoy long life. Hear, O Israel, and be careful to obey so that it may go well with you and that you may increase greatly in a land flowing with milk and honey, just as the Lord, the God of your fathers, promised you. Hear, O Israel: The Lord our God, the Lord is one. Love the Lord your God with all you heart and with all your soul and with all your strength. These commandments that I give you today are to be upon your hearts. Impress them on your children. Talk about them when you sit at home and when you walk along the road, when you lie down and when you get up. (Deuteronomy 6:1–7)

Notice that these commandments were so important to God that the health of the Israelites, and even the length of their life, depended on their diligence in keeping His laws. If God told you to do something, and you knew that whether you live or die depended on your response, what would you do? These were important words indeed.

These verses are often used to emphasize the need to train our children spiritually in the home. But notice that the primary focus of these verses is the personal call to love God with everything that you have. It is only when we accept this challenge that we are able to pass these truths on to our kids in an authentic way. We need to be models before we can be effective teachers.

No amount of spiritual talk will speak more loudly than our life. Children are incredibly perceptive, and they know if what we say matches who we are and what we do. And if what we live and what we say do not match up, they will believe what we live, not what we say.

Owning a relationship with your God is a prerequisite to impacting your children in a way that honors Him. If we live godly lives, then we can teach godly lessons. We are to impress God's commands on our children.

MAKING AN IMPRESSION

Children are like Play-Doh®, that colorful, clay-like substance. When our children were much younger, they would spend hours molding the dough into various shapes. If you can keep the stuff out of their hair and food, it's a great way for them to express their creativity. Early on kids learn that if they take objects and press them into the Play-Doh, it will leave an exact impression of the object. Over time, the Play-Doh will harden and whatever image has been impressed into it becomes set.

In a sense, through the years your son has been the Play-Doh and you have been the object. The impression that you have made, and continue to make in him through the thousands of things that you say and do, will eventually become set, difficult to change. Interestingly, when Moses called the family to "impress [the commandments] on your children" (Deuteronomy 6:7), he used the Hebrew word for "impress" that carries this same meaning—to strike deep into the mind and hearts of the children, like an object striking into pliable clay.

With this in mind, let's consider two key truths about the model that you present to your son:

1. You are making an impression.
2. You cannot make an impression of something you don't have.

1. You Are Making an Impression

Jerry never set out to mold his son, Greg, into anything special. Their corner grocery store had been in the family for years, and Greg grew up spending lots of time working side by side with his dad. But the family business was not the only thing Greg learned from his dad—he also learned Dad's values.

One day as Jerry was restocking some shelves, he noticed Greg running out the door, leaving the cash register unattended. When his son returned, Jerry gave him a mini-lecture about responsibility. When he finished, he asked Greg why he had run from the store.

THE GREAT IMPRESSION

"Well, that older lady who was just in here paying for her groceries dropped a twenty-dollar bill when she opened her purse, and I didn't notice it on the floor until after she left. I was trying to catch her to give it back to her."

Too bad Jerry didn't ask why he left before he gave his mini-lecture! You see, Greg had grown up watching his father run an honest business. There were plenty of opportunities to cheat customers out of change and to be dishonest with prices, but Jerry would have none of it. As a Christian businessman who desired to serve Christ, Jerry was more concerned with his honesty and his witness than with his profits. In actions and well as words, the impression that Jerry made in the clay of Greg's life had taken hold. As a result, the twenty-dollar bill that would have been easy for Greg to stick in his own pocket ended up back in the lady's purse.

Unfortunately, not all of the impressions we make are positive. It can be scary how much like us our sons often are. They may walk like us, talk like us. If you like a certain sports team, so will they. If you belch at the table, so will they. If you read your Bible, so will they. (Although the push for independence that comes with adolescence may obscure these similarities at times.)

What does your son see you get excited about? Are you excited about worshiping your Lord, or is fishing at your favorite lake more important to you? Do you get irritated with the pastor when his sermon runs long and you miss the first quarter of the football game? There is nothing wrong with heading out to fish at your favorite lake, or teeing up a ball at the golf course, or watching a football game on the tube. But remember that your priorities in life, the things you spend your time with, the things that give you the most satisfaction—all of these are making an impression in the soft clay of your son's life. How does your walk with Christ and your interest in spiritual growth stack up with your other activities?

Do not make the mistake of thinking that you do not make much of a difference in your son's life. You do, like it or not. The question is not if you will make an impression, but what impression you will make. Joseph Nowinski has stated,

> Teenage boys borrow bits and pieces of their emerging identity
> from their fathers, often without acknowledgment or even aware-
> ness. . . . Many key attitudes toward work, authority, relation-
> ships, and self are adopted from our fathers during adolescence.
> This typically goes on beneath a veneer of rebellion, which in

boys reflects their ongoing need to be different from their erst-while models and therefore individual. At heart, however, fathers and sons are cut from the same cloth much more than they might like to think.[4]

2. *You Cannot Make an Impression of Something You Don't Have*

Give a child a dime and ask him to make an impression of a quarter in his Play-Doh. Of course, it can't be done. To make an impression of a quarter, you need a quarter. We can only make an impression with what we have. The impression we make as a dad is who we are—the good and the bad.

Do you want your son to live a godly life of integrity, loving the Lord with all his heart, soul, and strength? Then show it to him in your life. If that's what you want to impress on his life, then with God's help you need to develop it in yourself. He may not know it, but your son is counting on you.

Ken Canfield, known for his research on fathering, comments on your power as a father:

> You have power. Your very presence among your children will affect their spiritual views. You don't even have to open your mouth to fulfill a part of your equipping role. You are the most important man in the world to them. The simple fact that you own a Bible is communicating something valuable to your kids. Of course, owning a Bible but not reading it is also communicating something powerful. You have power as a father. Use it positively.[5]

Too many books on parenting try to teach us how to help our children become something that we have not been able to develop in our own lives. Do you want your children to spend time reading God's Word? Develop the discipline of reading it yourself. Do you want your children to be honest, kind, responsible? Work on those areas in your own life. Be careful with the impressions that you make.

Modeling Integrity

So what does a dad who wants to be a godly role model for his son look like in everyday life? What marks his life, what qualities does he have, what does he do?

The answer to these questions can be summed up in one word—integrity. The word means wholeness in person and in deed, or as Webster's defines it, being in an "unimpaired or unmarred condition."[6] Proverbs 20:7 (NASB) tells us that "a righteous man who walks in his integrity—how blessed are his sons after him." Integrity is the stuff that allows us to relate to God, to others, and with ourselves in ways that are unimpaired. A righteous man of integrity has relationships that are authentic, genuine, and honest. He does not pretend to be something he is not.

An Honest Pastor

Charles Stanley, pastor of the First Baptist Church of Atlanta, successful author, and internationally known and respected for his "In Touch" radio program, is generally regarded as a godly leader. When Stanley spoke in November 1992 at an international meeting of Christian counselors, he surprised many in the audience with a confession of his struggles and shortcomings. He talked about the emotional baggage that he brought into his ministry—hostility, poor self-image, rebellion. He disclosed how his stepfather had contributed to the flaws that he saw in himself as an adult. "When it came to a sense of worthiness, he absolutely destroyed everything in me that thought I was worth anything."

As Stanley poured out his heart in describing how God had helped him to overcome his past, he concluded, "There are a whole lot of fellas out there like me, who are hurting worse than I've hurt."[7]

Maybe you are one of those "fellas out there" who is hurting. You know you're not what you want to be, but you struggle with attitudes and behaviors that seem to get in the way of loving God and relating with your family in healthy ways. You're imperfect.

No Need to Be Perfect

Well, take heart, dad—integrity is not the same as perfection. Furthermore, God does not ask you to be perfect, without sin. If you feel that you don't measure up, you are in good company. Dr. Stanley has been there, and so have we. We are convinced that all fathers feel inadequate at times. But we are still qualified to lead our sons. You are the right man to lead your boy.

The pursuit of righteousness and integrity is a lifelong pursuit—but we need to be pursuing it. The tragedy is when we allow those thoughts of past failures to keep us from growing into who God wants us to be.

Integrity can be a tough concept to pin down, so let's look at some characteristics and behaviors that can help us to get a handle on it.

THE GREAT IMPRESSION

A righteous man of integrity:

- Seeks to place God first in his life.
- Is willing to take an honest look at himself in light of God's standards.
- Recognizes his strengths and his weaknesses.
- Is real and loving in his relationships with others.
- Spends time and energy in serving others, including his family.
- Takes responsibility for his actions.
- Actively permits himself to be held accountable to at least one other man.
- Admits when he is wrong.
- Is not afraid to be vulnerable, letting others see him as he really is.
- Is a man of his word—he keeps his promises.

We need more models of integrity. From government officials to church leaders to everyday people we pass on the street, society is filled with people who lack integrity. As a result, people of real integrity shine like beacons in a dark world. Men of integrity think, feel, and express themselves deeply.

"A real man must not be afraid to tell you who he is deep down inside," explains Stu Weber. "[The apostle] Paul describes a form of communication that reaches back, back, behind the rib cage. It's a vulnerable, wide-open, unselfish, 'here is my soul' communication."[8]

One of the best things you can do for your son is to provide him with a model of godly integrity. Who you are as a man is far more powerful than any advice you will ever give to him. As we have seen, a real man of integrity does not need to be perfect or pretend that he is. In fact, just the opposite is true. A real man of integrity acknowledges that he is fallen and sinful, and that it is only by the grace of God that he can become what God wants him to be. He relates to his family in ways that are loving and genuine. Such a man is respected and admired, not scorned and ridiculed. Any son would be proud to have such a man for a father.

A MODEL FOR A LIFETIME

George Jaeger, his father, and three young sons were enjoying their New England fishing trip in the Atlantic. Grandpa and the boys were

THE GREAT IMPRESSION

enjoying themselves as much as George, laughing and talking and reeling in some big ones. Late afternoon they started the boat engine and headed for home. The waters were becoming choppy, but they looked forward to a fun drive back home in the car.

After only a few miles, though, the outboard engine sputtered and quit, and to their dismay, the boat started to take on water. The increasing winds piled the waters into large waves, and the water began to fill the boat. The Jaegers did everything they could think of, bailing water and looking for another boat to hail, but it became apparent that the boat was going to sink.

With no other options, they tightened the buckles on their life jackets, linked themselves together with a rope, and plunged into the dark, cold Atlantic water. George had glanced at his watch as they entered the water and the boat disappeared—6:30 P.M.

Little was said between them in order to save energy, and soon darkness enveloped them. The Jaegers were trying to swim and float for the shoreline, though George suspected it was many hours away. He reminded the boys not to drink the ocean water, but the choppy sea forced the salt water against their mouths. First one boy, then another, swallowed too much salt water. One by one they gagged and strangled as they fought to keep their heads up.

Their helpless father heard his sons, one by one, and then his own father, choke and drown. Refusing to surrender, George continued to try and make his way to land. After eight exhausting hours, he staggered onto the shore, still pulling the rope that bound him to the bodies of the other four.

"I realized they were all dead, my three boys and my father. My youngest boy, Clifford, was the first to go. I had always taught our children not to fear death because it meant being with Jesus. Just before he died, I heard him say, 'Goodbye, dad, I'd rather be with Jesus than go on fighting.'"[9]

In those dark and terrible hours, George Jaeger had the chance to witness the impact, the impression, of his fifteen years as a father. His boys died quietly, with courage and dignity. Up to the very last minute, one by one they modeled the truth that had been passed on to them by their dad.

Reading George's story, I thought, *What an awful feeling to helplessly watch your sons die. How would I react in such a situation? Would I panic? Would I curse God?* I ask you the same questions: How would you react in such a crisis? What kind of model would you be in those last moments?

THE GREAT IMPRESSION

"Impress [God's principles] on your children," Moses commanded. As dads, we must remember that we best impress them through a consistent, godly example, through good times and bad. Remember, as models to our children, we run in a marathon, not a sprint: We must live consistent lives, not a quick burst of good intentions every now and then. Our lives should be "full-time" examples to our sons. We cannot throw in a Bible verse here and there, spend a few minutes with our son now and then, or work at being "dad for a day" and expect that those moments will be sufficient to carry our son to godly maturity.

Like a marathon runner, there will be times when we stumble and fall, but we need to pick ourselves up and fight the temptation to give in. The finish line is years ahead, but the thrill of persevering and completing the race is well worth it. A man of vision and integrity sees that and pushes ahead.

FIFTEEN
WORKING YOUR WAY OUT OF A JOB

L eading your son from boyhood to manhood is seldom smooth. As Don and Jeanne Elium, co-authors of *Raising a Son: Parents and the Making of a Healthy Man,* emphasize, "Maturation in males is often slow, painful, and messy."[1]

For your son, this is a time of letting go of the safe and comfortable role of child, striking out on his own. He is in search of his identity as a man, a person, and a follower of Christ. His choices are often attempts to "test the waters" of autonomy, or sometimes even to make a statement that tells the world that, right or wrong, the time has come to "live my own life." This is healthy and normal. For your son, it's also scary and lonely.

For you as a parent of an adolescent boy, the pain is usually more subtle, more deliberate. The feeling of loss that comes with an adolescent's transition into adulthood sneaks up on most parents. A father may experience a quiet tug of sadness and emptiness, but for the most part the years are too active, and sometimes too volatile, to reflect on the process. It may seem as if one day your son started to speak and you had little time to think about that, for before you knew it he was arguing with you. Now he talks all the time about his plans, or he writes essays for class. The old, worn-out cliché that kids grow up too fast hits you right between the eyes. The tears may be hidden deep within your heart, acknowledging the sadness of loss.

No, you are not losing your son. But when adolescence appears, you are losing your little boy. This is the same baby who squealed with

WORKING YOUR WAY OUT OF A JOB

delight when you tossed him into the air. The toddler who loved to crawl up into your lap, just to cuddle. You taught him how to ride a bike, throw a baseball, and bait a hook. He needed you then, dad. He needs you now. He needs you to be a friend, a coach, a confidant. While the feelings of loss are real, it is helpful to recognize that the next stage of being a parent is every bit as precious, rewarding, and fun as previous stages. It is time to celebrate your son becoming a man.

WEAVING A RELATIONSHIP

There is an advantage to understanding the stages of adolescence, knowing what's coming next, and having some specific ideas, rites, and rituals that help to bring your son to maturity. This book, like many others, can be helpful in sorting out the various issues your son will face as he grows up. But we must remember that reading books is no substitute for developing the understanding and the kind of relationship with your son that allows him to make a healthy transition from boy to man. You're working on maintaining the level of trust with your son during this transition period, and that's a learning process with starts and stops, successes and setbacks.

Parenting is the purest as well as most base form of leadership, and "leadership is more a weaving of relationships than an amassing of information."[2] Knowing what your son is going through, and living—even celebrating—it are two very different things.

This "weaving of relationship," then, is the essence of parenting an adolescent boy. Your goal is to work yourself out of a job—the job of delivering your son to the threshold of godly manhood. Fathering means to raise a son to independent self-identity as a man. How do you do that? The key is building on a relational foundation with your son, using six tools of the fathering trade: (1) model devotion to Jesus, (2) pass on a legacy, (3) develop his decision-making skills, (4) handle the fine art of discipline, (5) develop the art of communication, and (6) call him to integrity.

Drawing on your friendship, the time you spend together, and your willingness to learn and grow as a father will enable you to give your son the very best opportunity to become the man God has created him to be. These six components will help you to build on this relational foundation.

SIX COMPONENTS OF EFFECTIVE FATHERS

1. Model Devotion to Jesus
The previous chapter highlighted the incredible power of the model we as fathers give to our sons. Our sons will repeat what we say, but

they will live like we live. If we say we are Christians, they will usually respond in kind. But if we profess a belief system that is followed up by a lifestyle that ignores or denies the sacrificial reality of faith in Christ, what we verbally teach our sons will have little value.

Sure enough, as soon as you deride your son for yelling "You jerk!" to a neighbor kid, he will ask, "Why, then, Dad, did you call that guy on your tail a jerk last night in the car?" Though our initial response may be to invoke the standard, traditional parental cop-out—"That's different!"—or even "Do as I say, not as I do!" inside we know better. Lines like those, in fact, must have first been blurted out by a father who knew he was wrong but somehow couldn't face up to it with his son. Sometimes the things we say make little objective sense, but we fathers have the spiritual gift of making self-serving platitudes sound like pearls of wisdom. When a son figures this out, however, the result is that we mold a monster who looks just like us.

This is true of our spiritual life as well. As Dave Veerman points out,

> Whether you like it or not, your life is the first Bible most people ever read. That is why Jesus taught that our lives must be dominated by His love, not by religious activity alone. Our sociology must reflect our theology. How you treat people will be the clearest indication to them of who you really think God is.[3]

The most powerful influence in a child's spiritual life is the authenticity of the parent's faith. The most productive and effective way to help your son become a man who is committed to following Jesus Christ with integrity and depth is to guard your own life and faith. As you pray, confess sin, and ask and receive forgiveness, and as you honestly and openly seek to follow Christ with humility and passion, your son will be forever imprinted with that image. A godly man has the best chance to raise a godly son.

2. Pass on a Legacy

You may not be great at telling stories, but you can be a great family storyteller. In so doing, you will bind your family, especially your son (or sons) close to you. "[Family] stories aren't icing; they're basic ingredients in any group that claims to be family,"[4] declares Delores Curran, author of *Traits of a Healthy Family.*

Passing on fatherly wisdom via the telling of family history and stories seems out-dated and old-fashioned to the modern mind. You may remember some fun story-telling when you watched certain TV characters as a child—Sheriff Andy Taylor with Opie, and "Papa" Walton with his crew of six children—but you may also look at our sophisticated, technological, fast-paced world and conclude, "For a father to sit on a porch swing, arm around his son, telling him what it was like when he was a boy, what his dad used to say, and how he felt growing up feels so artificial and corny. Besides, I'm too busy, and my son's too busy. He doesn't want to sit and talk . . . those days are over."

But are they? Or, at the very least, can we make time to re-create them with our children? In every tribe, culture, and civilization one of the primary tasks of the elders in each family was to pass on the unique legacy and history of that family. In most cultures throughout the centuries the father has been given the task of passing on this history. In our culture it is more often the maternal side of the family that keeps up with extended family and maintains contact between disjointed and distant members. But, as important a role as this is, it is not the passing on of the family legacy. There needs to be more—kids need a connection to something larger than themselves.

Telling stories is not difficult, but it does not come naturally to most of us either. Though grandparents love to sit and tell stories, most parents don't. This may be due to a parent's fears, but it is mostly due to the busyness of life. But a great joy of being a parent is passing on to your children a sense of connectedness, and a great way to do that is to take the time to tell stories.

Remember, your son is a product of generations who affect him even today. He needs the gift of family history. Whenever possible, tell your son something about your (and your wife's) parents and grandparents, your family memories, or anything that will help him connect with his legacy. Here are four natural times to tell certain family stories:

1. *At bedtime,* before you pray. Talk to him about your history.

2. *When he has made a comment that hits you as significant.* Stop then and connect it to family history. Sometimes we don't have the time to respond immediately with any depth, but be sure to come back to it to discuss it more fully in light of family history.

3. *At the "teachable moment."* At certain key times your son is receptive to hearing how you handled a given situation, or how your dad reacted when you brought home a bad grade.

4. *During vacation.* Vacations are markers that help define a family; therefore, they are great opportunities for passing on a family legacy by reflecting as a family about the past.

Again in this age of time management, it may feel like wasted time to spend minutes telling stories, singing songs, recalling past events, and discussing family history, but it is one of the greatest gifts you have to offer your son. In the turbulent waters of late and post adolescence, your son needs to know that he is not alone, that there is a family that will always stand with him. Yes, it is important to teach your son that Jesus is always with him and for him, but this truth is even more powerful and impacting when it is Jesus and the people God has used to shape and mold him into the man he is.

3. *Develop Decision-Making Skills*

The greatest challenge in rearing kids during the adolescent years is moving from control toward allowing a healthy sense of independence. Control is safer, easier, cleaner. After all, you love your son and you know what is best for him. That is a wise and important strategy when he is a preadolescent. But it is debilitating and even dangerous when dealing with an adolescent. The process of handing over control to your son must begin early on in his life, but your recognition of the importance of independence and autonomy is manifested when your son hits adolescence.

As hard as it is, a child's healthy development, and most especially faith development, is dependent on being taught how to make wise decisions. In so doing, he is able to move from parental control to self-control. "Children cannot be forced to be good—not indefinitely," wrote Martin R. DeHaan, Jr. "Overall, the Bible shows a mature approach to parenting will follow the example of the heavenly Father. He loved us as no other parent has ever loved, while also giving his children enough room to make their own choices and mistakes."[5]

In chapters 7, 10, and 13 we have provided several ideas and suggestions for giving your son increasing responsibility as he moves through the various stages of adolescence. These ideas, however, will have little effect if you as the parent do not emotionally and intentionally allow your son to fall on his face in order to learn a lesson. Yes, telling him stories about the time you crashed the car when driving across town may help to remind him to be cautious, but he must have the opportunity, and the accompanying trust, to go on his own. He may crash the car, he may make poor choices, and he definitely will fail at times. But this is vital for his growth into manhood—to experience failure while still under the security of your support and influence during his adolescent years.

If you as his father try to overly control him, even (from your perspective) for his own good, he will have to wait to experiment with life's choices when he is away from your parental influence. Then, when disappointment and failure come, he will not have you there to help him through the failure.

As a young camper, I (Steve) still remember the day that I made the mistake of giving my favorite horse, Star, too much slack in the reins. He sensed the unrestrained freedom that I was giving to him, and he took off at full speed. Almost without thinking, I pulled hard on the reins to get him to stop. Big mistake! The next thing I knew I was flying off Star's back. I ended up in bed with a bruised hip for almost a week.

The way I need to parent my sons is not unlike the way I needed to handle Star. They need to be able to discover who they are and be allowed to grow up. If we try to hold them back and control their every move—if we hold the reins too tight—we may succeed only in getting them to throw us off their back. The harder we pull the reins, the more they will resist.

It was a mistake to give Star complete freedom, and it was also a mistake to pull too hard on the reins. When he had complete freedom, I felt out of control. When I pulled too hard, he felt out of control. In both cases, we both did what we felt we needed to do to regain some control.

When I was willing to work with him rather than against him, Star cooperated with my directions. He allowed me to influence his path, and he took my guidance as long as I didn't pull the reins too tight.

Instead of trying to control and rein in your son, help him to learn how to weigh consequences when making choices. Issues like curfew, dating and friendship partners, homework, and extracurricular activities are all gifts to help your son learn how to make those choices that are the best for him and that reflect his faith. When he makes the decision, the outcome becomes all the more real and relevant to him.

4. Handle the Fine Art of Discipline

A dad must not shy away from proper discipline when a son intentionally disobeys. But what is proper discipline? Does it include physical force and pain, verbal threats, harsh language?

"Spare the rod, spoil the child," is an oft-quoted proverb typically used to make a case for corporal punishment. The problem is that it is not found in the Bible. However, several verses found in Proverbs having to do with discipline do include the word *rod*:

> He who spares the rod hates his son, but he who loves him is careful to discipline him. (13:24)

WORKING YOUR WAY OUT OF A JOB

Folly is bound up in the heart of a child, but the rod of discipline will drive it far from him. (22:15)

Do not withhold discipline from a child; if you punish him with the rod, he will not die. Punish him with the rod and save his soul from death. (23:13–14)

The rod of correction imparts wisdom, but a child left to himself disgraces his mother. (29:15)

In the great debate regarding the use of physical punishment in the disciplining of children, virtually no secular and few Christian psychologists advocate anything more than lightly spanking a young child (usually under the age of seven or so) to let him or her know you mean business. The emphasis in Proverbs 13:24 is not on the *mode* of discipline (the rod) but on the fact that discipline at times is necessary. This is in line with how many scholars view Proverbs 22:15 and 29:15, where the "rod of discipline" is used to draw a child away from "folly" and "impart wisdom." Here the rod is not so much an instrument of punishment as a metaphor for the necessity of discipline in rearing a child. Even Proverbs 23:13–14 indicates that the rod is a last resort form of discipline, one step before a child's behavior results in death.

There is no doubt that discipline is necessary in rearing sons. As the writer of Hebrews states, "If you are not disciplined (and everyone undergoes discipline), then you are illegitimate children and not true sons" (12:8). Whenever God's Word refers to this process as it relates to how He deals with His children, the word used is *discipline,* not *punishment.* Not so with those who are not his. After all, the goal of discipline is found in its root word—disciple. Through teaching, instruction, and correction our goal is to make disciples of our sons.

But what kind of discipline is important and valuable as a son goes through the adolescent years? The overall biblical requirement for fathers in dealing with their children, regardless of the offense, is found in Ephesians: "Fathers, do not exasperate your children; instead bring them up in the training and instruction of the Lord" (6:4). As you consider the proper method of punishment for a teenager, include the following five guidelines for appropriate discipline. (As guidelines, they are not necessarily right for every boy; they provide a starting point.)

1. *Stay calm.* This may be difficult to do, but avoid doling out consequences in the heat of an argument, or in the midst of a confrontation you may hear, "I don't care what you do to me!" Let your son

know that there will be consequences, but you both need a cooling-off period to make a decision as to what it will be.

2. *Look beyond your son's words and try to determine what is behind his behavior.* If you can stay calm, not overreacting to an immediate situation, but waiting for the facts to come out, you can help your son sort out for himself what other factors are affecting his behavior. This does not mean he can avoid discipline or consequences; it simply gives him the chance to look inside and determine why he lied or yelled or was irresponsible. This makes the disciplinary process a teachable moment and a growth opportunity, which is the ultimate goal of discipline anyway.

3. *Make the consequences fit the crime.* When we confine a fourteen-year-old to his room for an hour, for example, for mistreating his eight-year-old sister, to him this may be as much a reward as a punishment. Instead, have him do her chores for a day or help her organize her closet.

4. *Invite your son, when he is (relatively) rational, to choose his own consequences.* As risky as it sounds, as this strategy becomes similar to a family ritual, your son will most likely be harder on himself than you would have been. Yes, at times or seasons your son may try to take advantage of this, yet when he knows that he has some control over his life, even when he needs to be corrected, he has a foundation for learning the self-discipline he will need later in life.

5. *If possible, walk with him through the discipline.* If your son breaks a door frame by slamming his door harder than a godly person should, the consequence may be that he will have to arrange to have it repaired, and pay for it. To earn the money (maybe don't allow him to use allowance for this), he may take on some extra chores. Offer to work with him, not to ease his consequences, but to let him know that because you love him you want to serve him in the midst of his discipline.

5. The Art of Communication

The most frequent complaint of kids when it comes to their parents goes something like this: "They don't understand me!" The most frequent complaint of parents when it comes to their kids is "They never talk!" Parents think kids don't talk, and kids think parents don't care to understand them.

Don't

- Look away—or worse, walk away—while your son is speaking.
- Allow other family members, including your wife, to interrupt your conversation. If you do interrupt to talk to others, apologize and return your attention to him.
- Interrupt him while he's speaking.
- Correct him.
- Jump to conclusions before you fully understand his side of the story.
- Walk by him when you come home and not acknowledge him with a thoughtful comment and a willingness to listen if he has something to say.

Do

- Set aside several minutes each day to ask your son how his day went.
- Put down the mail or the paper when your son starts to speak to you.
- Look at your son when he speaks.
- Ask your son to expand whenever he makes a comment.
- Repeat back to him what he said, especially if you don't understand.
- Ask questions and listen to his answers before getting angry about something he did or said.
- Show him you care by nodding, smiling, and touching him when he discloses his thoughts and feelings.
- Tell him you love him.

In addition, the quality and depth of family communication depends on three "relational themes"—trust, confirmation, and openness. When these three themes are present in any relationship, but especially in a family, both individuals feel a connection. This connection is confirmed, organized, and experienced through communication.

You may not consider yourself very skilled at any one communicative skill (listening, giving feedback, and so on). Often a strong relationship of trust, openness, and confirmation will overcome much of those faulty messages and misunderstanding, because the two people (in this case, father and son) are willing to work through the issues.

Trust occurs when the person I am in relationship with has confidence in my integrity as a person. The degree to which I feel trusted is directly related to how much I am willing to reveal to the person. A father who has not developed a relationship based on mutual trust with his son can become an interpersonal communication expert and still never connect with his son in a meaningful way. Developing this trust is more a mind-set than a specific strategy, and telling your son you trust him is nothing compared to showing him that you trust his mind, his heart, and his character.

Openness, closely related to trust, is more easily measured and identified than trust. Openness describes the ease and flow of communication in the relationship. Is your dialogue with your son always superficial and forced? If so, this is a sign that you need to explore any areas where you may be hiding from each other. This must be mutual, for intimacy and self-disclosure is impossible one-way. Your son needs to know that you are being straight and free in your relationship with him, within appropriate boundaries, which are clearly communicated to him, in order to feel safe enough to shoot straight with you.

Confirmation is the quality that states, both in word and deed, that I, as your father, believe in you. I confirm your worth and value as my boy for who you are, versus who I have always wanted you to be. For many dads this is difficult, because as sons grow they need the freedom to be themselves instead of the boys their dads had always envisioned them to be. Your son may not be an athlete, a musician, or an engineer, but you need to continually confirm to him that you are proud of who he is, because he is your boy.

The rites of passage in this book are designed to do just that—give your son a sense of confirmation that he is now ready to move on in his journey toward manhood with all of the responsibility and individuality for which it calls.

6. *Call Him to Integrity*

In the previous chapter, we called dads to become models of integrity for their sons. Being men of integrity is fundamental to bringing sons to godly maturity.

Integrity is an inner quality that affects our outer deeds. It brings together all that a man is, from the inside out. In this compartmentalized, fragmented, and superficial culture, where men have learned to hide their feelings, carry incredible burdens, and stand alone in the face of a hostile world, integrity has taken a back seat. In nearly every business in this land, including the institutionalized church, power is often more highly prized than integrity. On the outside we are building our walls, boundaries and kingdoms, but on the inside we are running as fast as we can just to keep up.

Our sons, however, deserve better than to be handed a legacy of deceit, fear, compromise, and isolation. They must be taught that weakness is not failure and that even failure is a gift in the journey of life. To need relationships, to cry out for help, to weep at pain and sorrow, to share honestly with others the condition of a wounded heart is not to be any less of a man. These are the marks of a man of integrity, a man who recognizes that failure and loneliness and need and fear are the building blocks of faith.

A man of integrity is man enough to admit that he doesn't have all the answers. A man of integrity makes a promise intending to keep his word, even if it costs him dearly. A man of integrity admits failure and asks forgiveness when even his best intentions cannot or are not fulfilled; he picks himself up in the light of grace and forges ahead, learning from his defeats. A man of integrity is committed to the law of loving his neighbor as himself, whoever that neighbor happens to be. Most of all, a man of integrity loves Jesus Christ with passion, trusts Jesus Christ with fervor, and follows Jesus Christ with focused dedication.

Call your son to integrity. Invite him into the turbulent waters of faith as he grows up. Allow him to see you struggle with compromise and failure and arrogance and fear. Grant him permission to care for you when you are in need, without burdening him beyond what he can bear. Give him the gift of a father who is authentic, a dad who is more concerned with truth than personal acclaim. Pass on to your son the torch of faith in Jesus Christ, the "high priest whom we confess" (Hebrews 3:1).

APPENDIX
A WORD
TO MOTHERS

As we noted in the introduction, this book is designed for fathers. But clearly the mother's role is indispensable for the success of a family. Your son really needs your husband and you to be on the same page when it comes to helping him grow up. Your son needs to have both of you talking, sharing, and interacting with each other so that he experiences the security of a loving, united parental base of support. In other words, your son needs to see a healthy marriage in your home, where dad and mom invest themselves in loving each other and building warm relationships with their children.

Family research confirms that "adolescent self-esteem is related to family relationships,"[1] and yet it has not been discovered why or how this happens. The evidence pointing to the incredible force of a good marriage is compelling, yet there remains little hard data that helps us to understand why that is true. What is known is that a strong marriage is a consistent predictor of a child's self-esteem and overall health, and a great deal of evidence points to the back side of this same coin—a troubled marriage often produces troubled kids.

A Special Word to Single Moms

You may be a mother rearing your children alone. Be assured that God has not forgotten your needs or your love for your children, and He can help you rear spiritually strong sons. Divorce is not God's ideal, of course, yet there are ways you can help your son have a strong, positive male influence in his life. Most of all, you can be a strong godly influ-

A WORD TO MOTHERS

ence to him so that he will both respect girls, and later women, and cherish his own family ties.

The "Three Keys for Moms" that follow are for single mothers, too. They apply to you and whatever significant man is in your son's life. If his biological father is present and interested, the best thing you can do for your son is to encourage him to connect with his father. Avoid making your son's future your battleground—you all will lose, and for a very long time! Everything in this article can fit, even if you no longer live together as husband and wife.

If no father figure is available for your son, he still needs the life touch of an older man to help him become a man of integrity and promise. Do your best to find a man who will love him as a friend as well as a mentor. More than a role model, who shows your son how to live, he needs someone to walk beside him. Ask your church for help in this area. Though the church has been slow in recognizing and meeting this need, many local churches are trying to catch up. A youth pastor, while he most likely will have too many overall responsibilities to focus on one boy, can assist in finding and even training some men in your church to love your son.

However you approach meeting this crucial need in your son's life, never give up. Find your son a man he can look up to, share with openly and honestly, and connect with on a spiritual level. You may be the one to lead him through the rites of passage in this book, but he still needs a man to teach him what it means to be a man of integrity.

THE SHAPE OF YOUR MARRIAGE

What shape is your marriage in? You may classify it as good or in need of great repair. If you are a single parent, it is nonexistent. Single mothers must beware, as noted above, of speaking negatively of their ex-husband before their children. Within a marriage, both parents must seek for harmony. This is even more true with boys than with girls, especially when the boy reaches adolescence. Researchers Jouriles and Farris discovered that a parent's interaction with a son was more negative after marital conflict.[2] When a boy's parents are struggling, he receives a diminishing amount of clear communication and relational support. He may react in a variety of ways, but when a mom and dad are not together in rearing their son, he is the loser.

Mom, we believe that you want what we as authors want—warm, loving family relationships where dad and mom are both committed, with God's help, to doing the best job they can in rearing their son. We hope that the following information will help you to enable your hus-

A WORD TO MOTHERS

band and son to be all that God wants them to be. It takes teamwork to win as a family.

If you are a single mother, or in a step-parent situation, we want these suggestions to help you assist the man (or men) involved in your son's life. We believe it is important that you participate in the process we have described in this book. We hope you do.

THREE KEYS FOR MOMS

Key #1: Recognize and Acknowledge Your Own Feelings

Because of a variety of factors, somewhere deep inside you may be feeling uncomfortable or even insecure about the prospect of your son receiving so much attention from his father. What you are feeling is a natural expression of your development as a person. Not every woman will have such feelings, but if you do, be sure to acknowledge and deal with those feelings as your husband deepens his relationship with your son.

Beth soon felt left behind when her husband, Peter, was able to deepen his relationship with their oldest son. Beth was happy for the closeness Peter and Corey had: a strong father-son relationship now that Corey has entered midadolescence. But she also lamented, "I feel left out. Corey spends a lot of time with his friends, but when he is home, dad is number one. Peter and Corey do things together, go places, talk about life and girls and "man stuff," you name it. For twelve years or so Corey and I were so close—he'd tell me everything. I guess we're still close, but it's different. Now I find out about his life as much from his dad as I do from him."

Beth's experience is not unusual. When a son enters adolescence, two factors often converge at approximately the same time. For one thing, a son's attitudes, needs, and behavioral patterns change radically during this period. Second, his mother can find herself entering a mid-life period that brings probing reflection, emotional confusion, and concern over identity issues. This combination causes the most stressful time in the family life cycle, and it is where satisfaction with marriage and family is diminished. That is especially true when the first child—boy or girl—hits adolescence.

When a son enters the adolescent phase, there is a natural relational distancing from his mother that occurs. At the same time, the son begins to identify more closely with his father. That is the point of this book—to encourage fathers to take advantage of this God-given desire for a son to bond with his father during the adolescent period. If, even for a season, you struggle as a mother with your own sense of identity and worth, recognize that such distancing can cause a sense of emptiness and depression.

The encouraging news for a mother is that after a few years her son will emotionally return to her, while at the same time maintaining his connection to his father. This is the mark of a healthy man—a man who loves both his mother and father, but as two distinct people in his life. Understanding this can help you as his mother free him up to bond with his father, knowing that he must loosen his bonds with you for a season in order to become a healthy adult man.[3]

Key #2: Maintain Intimacy
with Both Your Son and Husband

Though your son may be getting closer to your husband, thus causing you to feel as if you are "losing" him, it is important for you to rise above this feeling and continue to be your son's friend. It is equally as important to encourage, support, and draw close to your husband. The fact is, moms are not left out, as Beth felt she was—they are still part of the team. But family relationships are transformed. You need to feel free to communicate your feelings and needs to your family, while also accepting that your son will never be your "little boy" anymore.

A mother who consciously commits to enabling the father-son relationship to develop greatly frees up both father and son to enjoy their relationship. As Stanley Cath, family researcher, states, "Fatherhood itself can only come into being and thrive with the mother's permission and support. How she introduces and conceptualizes her husband's role as father may be one of the most important determinants of how their child will relate to his father and to other men and women in later life."[4]

This is a season of life that can be extremely rewarding. As you encourage your husband and son to become closer friends, all the while maintaining your bond with both of them, you will find great joy in watching their relationship deepen and flourish. Your husband will be more fulfilled as a father, and your son will be growing into the man God created him to be. You are not losing him. You are watching your years of investment in him bloom, and that may be the greatest joy of motherhood.

A WORD TO MOTHERS

Key #3: Pray for
Your Husband and Son

In today's culture, where men are barraged with conflicting messages about what it means to be a successful husband, father, or even a successful man, your husband needs the clarity of purpose and hope only Jesus Christ can offer. He needs to sense God's call on his life to love his wife as Christ loves the church, to bring up his children in the nurture and admonition of the Lord, and to walk humbly with his God as a man of righteous integrity. That is not an easy task, and it requires the power of God to pull it off. If your husband is like most men, he will often feel insecure about his role as father as well as husband. Let him know that you are seeking God's guidance for him and that he can count on you to support and encourage him, especially in prayer.

Your son needs your prayers for different reasons. If you have read this book, you will recognize that a major component of adolescence is the need to establish his independence, rising above the need for his parents to control and regulate his life. Depending on how a family handles this need, it will inevitably cause some level of conflict. Your son may go through periods of struggle with your husband during these years, and at times they may be severe. Pray for your son's heart, that he will be open to his dad, that he will respect and look to his father for leadership, nurture, and encouragement. He needs to know, too, that you will be praying for him as he goes through adolescence. He needs to know that you are committing to the Lord his friendships, dating partners, schoolwork, and efforts to resist temptation and evil. It also sends a powerful message to your son to know that you are praying for his future spouse, whoever she may be, asking God to prepare her for your son and to keep her pure.

One note of caution: never, ever, use your commitment to pray for him as a tool to manipulate his behavior. Many kids have been pushed away from the Lord by well-meaning parents who in exasperation lash out, "I'm going to pray that you show some respect around here!" The last thing your son needs for his spiritual life is a prayer of intimidation.

Instead, during times of peace and calm, tell your son that you love him and are asking God to help him learn and grow through the teenage years, especially in his relationship to his father. Ask him what to pray for, and let him know this is your commitment of love to him.

Mothers have great insight and a tender love when it comes to their sons and daughters. Your prayers and active involvement in your son's life will strengthen him and encourage your husband.

NOTES

INTRODUCTION

1. David Heller, *Growing Up Isn't Hard to Do If You Start Out as a Kid* (New York: Villard, 1991), 234.

2. Ken Canfield, *The Seven Secrets of Effective Fathers* (Wheaton, Ill.: Tyndale, 1992), 193.

3. James Dobson, *Straight Talk: What Men Need to Know, What Women Should Understand* (Dallas: Word, 1991), 78–79. Clearly, as fathers we cannot guarantee that by offering the baton—the gospel—our sons will do their part in taking hold of it. Still, we must do our part in seeing to it that they have the chance.

4. Stu Weber, *Tender Warrior: God's Intention for a Man* (Portland, Ore.: Multnomah, 1993), 24.

5. Adapted from Ray Seilhamer, "A Vision Worth Living For," address given to Vision '94 Leadership Conference, Huntington, Indiana, August 1994.

CHAPTER 1: FOOTBALL, BASEBALL, AND RAISING BOYS

1. Gary Cartwright, "The Hungriest Coach," *Texas Monthly* (September 1992): 163.

2. Steve Buckley, "The Happiest Man in America?" *Sport* (July 1993): 26, 28.

3. Ibid., 28.

4. Tim and Christine Burke, *Major League Dad* (Colorado Springs: Focus on the Family, 1994), 5.

5. Ibid., 241, 247.

6. Foster Cline and Jim Fay, *Parenting Teens With Love And Logic* (Colorado Springs: Pinon, 1992), 96.

7. Stu Weber, *Tender Warrior: God's Intention for a Man* (Portland, Ore.: Multnomah, 1993), 145.

8. Ken Canfield, *The Seven Secrets of Effective Fathers* (Wheaton, Ill.: Tyndale House, 1992), 52.

Chapter 2: Growing Up Male in Tomorrow's World

1. David Howard, *How to Get Your Teenager to Talk to You* (Wheaton, Ill.: Youth for Christ, 1986), 11.

2. Gary Oliver, *Real Men Have Feelings Too* (Chicago: Moody, 1993), 54.

3. John Naisbitt and Patricia Aburdene, *Megatrends 2000* (New York: William Morrow, 1990), 11.

4. Princeton Religious Research Center, using statistics from a Gallup survey commissioned by CBN (May 1989). For more info, write CBN, CBN Center, Virginia Beach, VA 23463.

5. As cited in Dennis Byrne, "Requiem for Harriet, Non-PC Mom," *Chicago Sun-Times*, 6 October 1994, 27.

6. Ibid.

7. Ted Bowman, "The Father-Son Project," *Families in Society* 74 (1993): 22–27.

Chapter 3: Faith and Your Son

1. "Youthworker Roundtable: Constructing a Theological framework for Spirituality," *Youthworker Journal* 3 (Spring 1986): 52–51.

Chapter 4: Family Rites and Rituals

1. Ray Raphael, *The Men from the Boys: Rites of Passage in Male America* (Lincoln, Neb.: Univ. of Nebraska, 1988), xi, 5.

2. The reaction of one American man to primitive rites of passage (from ibid., xi.).

3. Delores Curran, *Traits of a Healthy Family* (Minneapolis: Winston, 1983), 210, 216.

4. Anthony Campolo, *Who Switched the Price Tags?* (Waco, Tex.: Word, 1986), 141–42, 144.

5. Raphael, *The Men from the Boys*, 12–13.

6. Gary Smalley and John Trent, *The Blessing* (Nashville: Nelson, 1986), 220–22.

7. Edwin Friedman, *Generation to Generation: Family Process in Church and Synagogue* (New York: Guilford, 1985), 164.

8. Gary Smalley and John Trent, *The Hidden Value of a Man* (Colorado Springs: Focus on the Family, 1992), 121, 123–24.

Chapter 5: Mental Notes: Ages 10–13

1. K. Chesto, "F.I.R.E. (Family-Centered Intergenerational Religious Education): An Alternative Model of Religious Education," D.Min. thesis, Hartford Seminary, 1987; cited in Kenneth E. Hyde, *Religion in Childhood and Adolescence: A Comprehensive Review of the Research* (Birmingham: Religious Education, 1990), 234.

2. Peter Benson, Dorothy Williams, and Arthur Johnson, *The Quicksilver Years* (New York: Harper & Row), 122.

Chapter 6: Parents, Peers, and (Gulp!) Puberty

1. Adapted from Anne Petersen, "Those Gangly Years," in *Human Development 91/92*, ed. Larry and Judith Fenson (Guilford, Conn.: Dushkin, 1991), 174–78.

2. Ibid., 182.

3. Patricia East, "Early Adolescents' Perceived Interpersonal Risks and Benefits," *Journal of Early Adolescence* 9 (1989): 374–95.

4. Petersen, "Those Gangly Years," in *Human Development 91/92*, 177.

5. Bruce Baldwin, "Puberty and Parents," in ibid., 183–87. Baldwin actually mentions two other emotions as well: personal hurt and pride.

6. Many parents find that a pleasant surprise awaits when they reveal their feelings of inadequacy to their teens. If the parent-child relationship is warm and healthy, the teen will often find ways to offer some encouragement and support. Being real and vulnerable with your son will draw you closer to each other—after all, you're only sharing with him what he has a good sense of already.

Chapter 7: The Early Adolescent Playbook

1. Due to a variety of factors, this scenario may not be an accurate depiction of your son. It is a generalization, useful for a comparison with other peiods of the developmental process. Every child will go through different issues at different times, and this generalization should not cause concern over how "normal" your son is.

2. Anthony Campolo, *Who Switched the Price Tags?* (Waco, Tex.: Word, 1986), 135.

Chapter 8: Mental Notes: Ages 13–15

1. John Janeway Conger, *Adolescence and Youth* (New York: Harper Collins, 1991), 146.

2. Adapted from David Elkind, *All Grown Up and No Place to Go* (Reading, Mass.: Addison-Wesley, 1984), 28–42.

3. John P. Hill, "Research on Adolescents and Their Families," in *Adolescent Social Behavior and Heatlh*, ed. Charles E. Irwin, Jr. (San Fransisco: Jossey–Bass, 1987), 15.

4. Elkind, *All Grown Up*, 41.

Chapter 9: Different Is Dangerous

1. Adapted from Bruce Baldwin, "Puberty and Parents," in *Human Development 90/91*, ed. Larry and Judith Fenson (Guilford, Conn.: Dushkin, 1991), 176–77.

2. Steve Dennie and Rob Suggs, *Murphy's Laws of Parenting* (Downers Grove, Ill.: InterVarsity, 1994).

3. John P. Hill, "Research on Adolescents and Their Families: Past and prospect," in *Adolescent Social Behavior and Health*, ed. Charles E. Irwin, Jr. (San Francisco: Jossey-Bass, 1987), 14–15.

4. F. Philip Rice, *The Adolescent* (Boston: Allyn & Bacon, 1990), 358.

5. Adapted from Baldwin, "Puberty and Parents," in *Human Development 91/92*, 183–87.

Chapter 11: Mental Notes: Ages 16–18

1. John Flavell, *Cognitive Development* (Englewood Cliffs, N.J.: Prentice-Hall, 1977), 125.

2. James E. Marcia, "Identity in Adolescence," in *Handbook of Adolescent Psychology*, ed. Joseph Adelson (New York: John Wiley & Sons, 1980), 159–87. In this pioneering work on identity statuses, Marcia labels the four types of identity *diffused, foreclosed,*

moratorium, and *achievement*; for this book I have called the four types *avoiding, settled, searching,* and *achieved.*

3. Tom Bisset, *Why Christian Kids Leave the Faith* (Nashville: Nelson, 1992), 103.

4. Ibid, 103.

Chapter 12: Social Curves

1. Mihaly Csikszentmihalyi and Reed Larson, *Being Adolescent* (New York: Basic Books, 1984), 9.

2. As cited in Diane E. Papalia and Sally Wendkos Olds, *A Child's World* (New York: McGraw-Hill, 1990), 575–76.

3. F. Philip Rice, *The Adolescent* (Boston: Allyn & Bacon, 1990), 363.

4. John P. Roche, "Premarital Sex: Attitudes and Behavior by Dating Stage," in *Adolescent Behavior and Society*, ed. Rolf Muuss (New York: McGraw-Hill, 1990), 235–43.

5. Josh McDowell, *Why Wait?* (San Bernardino, Calif.: Here's Life, 1987), 99.

6. Adapted from F. Philip Rice, *The Adolescent* (Boston: Allyn & Bacon, 1990), 432–33.

7. Mihaly Csikszentmihalyi, Kevin Rathunde, and Samuel Whalen, *Talented Teenagers: The Roots of Success and Failure* (New York: Cambridge Univ. Press, 1993), 154.

8. See E. Greenberger and L. Steinberg, *When Teenagers Work* (New York: Basic Books, 1986).

Chapter 13: The Late Adolescent Playbook

1. For information on S.H.A.P.E., write Saddleback Community Church, Attn.: Doug Fields, 23456 Madero, Suite 100, Mission Viejo, CA 92691. In addition, your church may have an instrument they use in a new believers or new members class. Ask for two copies to use at home.

Chapter 14: The Great Impression

1. Fran Sciacca, "Back to the Real Future" in *What Makes a Man?* ed. Bill McCartney (Colorado Springs: NavPress, 1992), 222.

2. Adapted from Jasper Abraham Huffman, *Building a Christian Home* (Winona Lake, Ind.: Light & Life, 1951).

3. "People," *Milwaukee Journal*, 4 February 1990, sec. 1.

4. Joseph Nowinski, *Hungry Hearts: On Men, Intimacy, Self-Esteem, and Addiction* (New York: Lexington, 1993), 71–72.

5. Ken Canfield, *The Seven Secrets of Effective Fathers* (Wheaton, Ill.: Tyndale, 1992), 179.

6. *Webster's Third New International Dictionary* (Springfield, Mass.: Merriam-Webster, 1986).

7. Charles Stanley, videotape recording, plenary session of International Congress on Christian Counseling, Atlanta, 13 November 1992.

8. Stu Weber, *Tender Warrior: God's Intention for a Man* (Portland: Multnomah, 1993), 77–78.

9. Adapted from Gordon MacDonald, *The Effective Father* (Wheaton, Ill.: Tyndale, 1981), 13–14.

NOTES

CHAPTER 15: WORKING YOUR WAY OUT OF A JOB

1. Don and Jeanne Elium, *Raising a Son: Parents and the Making of a Healthy Man* (Hillsboro, Ore.: Beyond Words, 1992), 81.

2. Princeton Religious Research Center, using statistics from a Gallup survey commissioned by the Christian Broadcasting Network (May, 1989). For more information, contact CBN, CBN Center, Virginia Beach, VA 23463.

3. David Veerman, *Youth Evangelism* (Wheaton, Ill.: Victor, 1988), 79.

4. Delores Curran, *Traits of a Healthy Family* (Minneapolis, Minn.: Winston, 1983), 202.

5. Martin R. DeHaan, II, "Radio Bible Class Discovery Series" (Grand Rapids, 1991), 12.

APPENDIX: A WORD TO MOTHERS

1. K. M. Galvin and B. J. Brommel, *Family Communication: Cohesion and Change* (San Francisco: Harper Collins, 1991), 220.

2. E. N. Jouriles and A. M. Farris, "Effects of Marital Conflict on Subsequent Parent-Son Interactions," *Behavior Therapy* 23 (1992). 370. When parents interacted with their sons after a marital conflict, the parents were more negative in three ways: (1) general communication suffered, (2) fathers delivered more demands to their sons that were vague and confusing, and (3) sons were less likely to comply with those commands.

3. For further discussion of the connection between raising a son through adolescence and the mother-father relationship, see Galvin and Brommel, *Family Communication*.

4. S. Cath, "Fathering from Infancy to Old Age: Toward a New Psychology of Men: Psychoanalytic and Social Perspectives," in *Psychoanalytic Review* 73, no. 4 (1986): 469–79.